Scenes From The Blue Book

Jeanette,

Thank you again for
supporting you cousin. I
hope you enjoy these words
God Bless

Kelly

Also by Kelly R. Jackson

Temporarily Disconnected

A perspective on the decline of Black relationships and families

Scenes From The Blue Book

Poetry, Reflection and the Spoken Mind

Kelly R. Jackson,
Author of *Temporarily Disconnected*

iUniverse, Inc.
New York Lincoln Shanghai

Scenes From The Blue Book
Poetry, Reflection and the Spoken Mind

iUniverse books may be ordered through booksellers or by contacting:

iUniverse
2021 Pine Lake Road, Suite 100
Lincoln, NE 68512
www.iuniverse.com
1-800-Authors (1-800-288-4677)

ISBN: 978-0-595-44964-4 (pbk)

ISBN: 978-0-595-89283-9 (ebk)

Printed in the United States of America

For Mama.

Contents

SCENE FOUR—A MESSAGE TO MY PEOPLE: "I KNOW YOU'RE DOWN, BUT WHEN YOU GON' GET UP?"

SCENE FIVE—KJ'S INSPIRATION: CLOSING ACT

Acknowledgements

I'd like to acknowledge my dear mother, Mrs. Annie Jackson-Loritts, for once again believing in me. This poetry book was the one she always wanted me to do. I was able to convince her that my first book, *Temporarily Disconnected*, was more important and needed to come first. We made a deal and I kept my end of the bargain, ma. You now have your poetry book. It's my first, but it won't be the last. You believed I could do this long before I did, so I love you so very much and I thank you for supporting and believing in your baby boy.

To my brothers and sisters, thank you again for supporting me. You have done nothing but encourage me since finding out about my "secret" author aspirations. I hope I made you proud with first book and I want you all to know that you are appreciated.

To my son, Steffen, continue to be special and continue to make me proud. You're growing into a fine young man and I hope that I had something to do with that. Dad loves you.

Angie, your love and friendship are immeasurable. You've always supported me, even when I didn't think the words were good enough. As you know, it hasn't gone unnoticed, but this time, I decided it should be in print. You're the true definition of a friend and I'll always love you no matter how many states you put between us.

To all that supported my first project, thank you for the inspiration. I wondered if anyone cared to read what I had to say, and through your support, I found that they did. Hopefully, you'll be on board with this project as well, and hopefully, something in these poems will inspire you as you have inspired me. Enjoy.

Kelly

Introduction

I wasn't sure what I would say in this introduction. I should be better at this by now. After all, this is my second book, so I should know what I'm doing by now. But this is a different type of book than my first one. The poetry book is a book all its own. In a sense, there are way more chapters. Each poem represents a different movement. A different feel. There's a different mental and emotional time with each poem.

I didn't realize that this book would be so hard to publish. I thought Chapter 5 of *Temporarily Disconnected* would be the most personal thing I'd ever publish. But as I got closer to publishing this book, I realized that some of these poems would be much more personal. Although a lot of what's included here are taken from the stories of others, some of them are mine. And no, I will not give page and location. You'll just have to guess. Although, if you were there …

Anyway, as you've already noticed from the Table of Contents, I broke this book up into scenes. I'll explain that in a moment. As for the title of the book, I've always kept my poems in a notebook. My mother always wanted me to publish them, but I was never sure if I would. I just kept filling them away in the notebooks, occasionally pulling them out when someone wanted to read them or when one was needed for a special occasion. What was eventually revealed to me through my friends was the fact that the notebooks always tended to be blue. Anytime friends would visit me and ask for something to read, if they wanted to read poetry, they'd always say, "Let me read from the blue book". Isn't it nice to have a meaning attached to a title? Also, I often view my work as scenes from one's life. For example, the very first poem of the book is a special tribute to my mother that I wrote for her retirement dinner. Those are all the scenes she's represented in my life. The second is a poem about me and how some have viewed me. I can't say that it's all necessarily untrue. In fact, it may all be true. But I'm not afraid of mirrors, so I included it here.

The first half of the book covers love and all that comes with it. To paraphrase a line from the poem "All I Wanted", it covers "joy, sadness, love and madness". The second half covers life, spirituality and, once again, the conditions of our people. However, there isn't just poetry included in this book. There are also a few short stories and a couple of commentary pieces. I didn't want to just do poetry. I've always thought that my work should be different. There are a lot of things that I felt the need to speak on. Some I spoke on through poetry, and some I felt I needed to attack in a more traditional form. There's a tribute to my family, as well as the black family in general, and there's also a call for a change in the language that we as blacks share with one another. I won't spoil it in the intro, I'll just let you see for yourself when you get there.

Well, I've said all that needs to be said here. It's time to get to the poetry. Get yo' tissues and handkerchiefs out. Or cut some onions for all of you that are too hard to show emotion. I hope it makes you smile, I hope it makes you laugh, I hope it makes you cry, I hope it causes you to reminisce and reflect, but most of all, I hope it makes you think.

KJ

Scene One — Opening Act

A special tribute to my mother …

The Gardener

Thank God for my mom, the multi-faceted black woman
She wears many hats and does many good deeds
Yet, she wears no hat more important than gardener
Both planting and nurturing her seeds

There's my mom, the professional gardener
In her briefcase is wisdom and truth
"My job is my ministry", she says to me
As she molds the minds of the youth

There's my mom, the Christian gardener
Planting the Word of God as she goes
Leading us by example by giving to those less fortunate
Well aware that she'll reap what she sews

There's my mom, the education gardener
Pushing her seeds to do their best
Reminding all who'll listen to the sound of her voice
That education is the key to success

There's my mom the advisor and nurturer
Who counsels us on how we should live
Many tears have been shed on her very strong shoulders
As wise life direction she continues to give

There's my mom, the disciplinarian
Unimpressed when you decide to show out
Her punishments are stiff, and if you remain unaware
No rod will be spared in her house

There's my mom, the parent and grandparent
A more dedicated soul, you've never met
And though her other accomplishments are quite impressive
This is her most impressive performance yet

Mom, take a look around this room
And admire the garden you own
How blessed you must feel to see firsthand
How beautiful your garden has grown

But not as blessed as we should feel having you in our lives
A greater mentor we could've never known
And we should honor your work from this day forward
By re-planting the seeds that you've sewn

Gemini

I've been tryin' to get in touch with my inner Gemini
'Cause I see the similarities between him and I
Special baby boy 'cause his mama said so
Put the pen to the paper, now I'm ready to blow
And we'll keep this thing movin' 'til the world sings my song
And 'cause duality exists, we don't always get along
My conflicts are real, I'm tryin' to right my wrongs
So we write in third person when we can't get along
Arrogance is fleeting, but when put to the test
He won't hesitate to tell you that he's one of the best
Too brash or too confident, it's all the same
But at the end of the day, his humility reigns
Recognition of the gifts that God has bestowed
Is the only way the gifts can continue to flow
I pray to God every night that he lights our way
'Cause my dark side twin will try to lead me astray
When I drive the Big Dog he makes me drive too fast
He makes me lust for a girl that's much too fast
When I should be home, he keeps me out half the night
He uses four-letter words when we ain't been treated right
But when my dark side threatens to claim my soul
It's the strength of my character that takes control
We're tryin' to make it right before we get too old
We're tryin' our best to find the right body to hold
Embracing spirituality is what we must learn
As the dark side will lead to a permanent burn
Though our dark side tends to be a lot of fun
What you lose is most times worth more that what you've won
In the face of all that's wrong, we must take a stand
And build the foundation of a better man
Though duality exists, we must take control
While accepting that the two halves make us whole
Come to terms with who you are 'cause it's what you must do
And embrace the Gemini that exists in you

Scene Two—Infatuation: Is this love that I'm feelin'?

Nice

The Reality of You

I've dreamed a thousand dreams for you
For you, I've knelt in prayer
Many a night I've talked with God
Just wishing you were there

I've been let down by love before
So to my heart I say, "Be still"
My desire is to ask you to stay forever
My desire is that you'll say you will

I don't wish to capture your spirit
If your spirit longs to be free
I've reached the night time of my life
And I want you to walk with me

Through this garden that we call life
We'll walk hand in hand
I want you to see the man that I am
I want you to understand

That my thoughts of you have become clear
I'm no longer afraid to love you
I've seen you for what you are
I believe your heart is true

Meet me in the garden
So that I may touch your face
I'm ready to put my fears to rest
And feel the warmth of your embrace

Held captive in the moment
Of our embrace and eventual kiss
I let the waters of love wash over me
Until all of my fears are dismissed

As the moonlight shines down upon us
The atmosphere causes emotions to rise
And I've realized that the stars in the sky
Are no match for the sparkle in your eyes

One could only hope to find
This love that I've found so true
My suspecting heart has finally come to believe
The reality of you …

Guardian Angel

Always on your shoulder
Always standing near
Never a need to worry
Never a need to fear

I'll be your guardian angel
Protecting you from all harm
Shielding you from danger
Holding you in my arms

Never doubt my courage
I was sent by God to protect you
And I'll protect you from all evil doers
And from those that disrespect you

I'll be sure to show you love
When you're in need of affection
And if you're lost in the forest
I'll be your sense of direction

When Satan's chains have you bound
I'll fight to set you free
And when the darkness blinds you
I'll be your eyes so you can see

When life turns your fairy tale
Into a sad story
I'll be the one to remind you
Of our Father's glory

For as long as you keep your faith
There's nothing you can't do
Just keep your mind and your heart pure
And all your dreams will come true

And when this world tries to bring you down
And keep you in despair
Just look over your shoulder for your guardian angel
And you'll see me standing right there

24-Hour Blue

7 hours and 13 days
Those words have been said before
But what happens when after 24 hours apart
I feel you don't want me no more?

It started last night at 11:36
When we hung up the phone in anger
Now here it is, 11:36 the next night
And my heart says our love is in danger

The last 24 hours for me
Have been anything but the best
I've really got nothing accomplished
No work, no play, no rest

The only thing that I've done
Is try to figure out exactly when
The tables of love tuned on us
And reminisce on what might have been

The ocean of our love has run dry
Our sunshine has turned to showers
Or maybe those are tears flowing from my eyes
Let me tell you about my 24 hours

Hours 1 through 8 were spent
In denial about how I felt
Simply telling myself over and over again
To play the cards that life has dealt

Besides, if she doesn't want you, let her go
You don't need her if she don't need you
But by the time hour 9 had rolled around
I found myself still blue

Hours 9 though 13 were spent
Using television to divert my attention
Knowing damn well if someone said your name
My heart would break at the mere mention

By hour 14 I had become frustrated
When it came to thoughts, you were my brain's only choice
I spent the next 60 minutes hoping the phone would ring
And on the other end would be your voice

When that didn't happen, I decided
That maybe some sleep was needed
But from hour 15 to 17 my brain betrayed me
For every dream of you, it received it

Hours 18 though 20 are a blur
Although I remember that my frustration grew
But I'm willing to bet a million dollars
I spent them pining over you

21, 22 and 23
Were spent avoiding all love songs
Whether happy, sad or otherwise, I avoided them
I just wanted to know what went wrong

'Cause there was a time when we were happy
There was a time when you treasured me
There was a time when I worshiped you
A time when we wanted to be

Much more that just a chapter
In the book of each other's lives
We wanted our love to grow each day
To do more that just survive

Now, instead of holding you in my arms and making up
I'm not exactly sure what to do
So I spent all of hour 24
Just writing these words to you

Surely

Last night, as I lay in bed, I received a revelation.
I was inspired to write it down.
I must tell you about my love for you.
Surely you've heard this before.
Surely there have been many before me.
Surely an angel like you has many, so many, that will tell you how they can't live without you.
Surely they tell you how your eyes shine brighter than the brightest of the stars in the sky.
They must have told you how you haunt them in their dreams each night. You must know how their hearts beat for you and only you.
Surely they all want to spend the rest of their days with you.
Surely they want to spend the rest of their nights with you.
Surely, but surely, your touch must set them all afire.
Your body must be all that they desire.
Your kiss must be the sweetest of all kisses to them.
But surely your eyes don't pierce their souls the way that they pierce mine. Surely they don't miss you when you're gone quite the way that I do. Surely their hearts don't ache for you quite the way mine does.
Surely you don't mean the world to them the way that you do to me. Surely, but surely, they don't see their unborn children when they look into your eyes the way that I do.
Surely they don't connect with your soul the way that I do.
Surely they don't desire to be your sun the way that I do.
Surely they don't desire for you to be their earth as I do.
Surely, but certainly, they don't love you as deep as I do.
With everything that I have.
To the depths of my soul.
With all that God will allow me to give.
Surely they don't love you as deep as I do.

Erykah and Amel

Thinking of a plan to win you over
Motivation hits my pen like a supernova
How can I be your man when you don't notice me?
Is this love that I'm feelin'? Quite possibly
I become a ball of nerves when there are thoughts of you
Can't believe how strong this has become, this crush I have on you
Stronger than the crush I have on Erykah Badu
Stronger than my crush on Amel Larrieux
This crush doesn't exist in the physical sense
'Cause my mind is too open, no longer dense
I first fell for Erykah 'cause she spoke the truth
I felt emotion from every word that she sang from the booth
I could feel it in my soul, what she says is true
And I feel the same things whenever I'm near you
Your smile is like warmth on the coldest night
And your touch is like magic and makes my heart takes flight
Causes the mind to race until I don't know what to do
Can't believe how strong this feeling's become, this crush I have on you
Stronger than my crush on Erykah Badu
Stronger than my crush on Amel Larrieux
When I first heard Amel, she touched my soul
Possessing the spirit of the young, with great reverence for the old
Beauty personified with an angelic voice
You're forced to give in to her rhythm and rhyme, 'cause your body no longer has
a choice
That's exactly how I feel whenever I'm in your space
Just can't control the uncontrollable desire to put my hands around your waist
But I'm getting too old for crushes and love letters are so high school
This is much stronger than what I felt for Erykah and Amel
I think I'm in love
In love
In love
I think I'm in love with you

Coffee Shop

I see her every Saturday at this downtown coffee shop. It's like it's become our own little ritual. Or maybe just mine. Every Saturday, at around 11am, I arrive. She's usually there already, but on occasion, my excitement leads me to beat her to the spot. Her skin is as brown as the coffee they serve, with just the right amount of cream. I've noticed her shoulder length black hair, though I've never seen her without her hat on. It's almost as if God has told her that I have a very special attraction to women in hats. She has a body sculpted to perfection, or at least what I consider perfection. Though we sit rather far apart, I've noticed her dark brown eyes. I'm usually reading my paper, and on occasion she'll be reading some beauty magazine, as if she needs to look any further than the closest mirror to define beauty.

On occasion, we've exchanged glances. There have even been times where she's smiled at me while looking over the rim of her coffee cup filled with cappuccino. Her smile cuts through me like a hot knife through butter. But in a good way. It's a smile that's way too special. It accents the cute little freckles on her nose, and causes her eyes to light up even more. And it causes me to melt inside like that aforementioned butter. Whenever I see it, it's like it cleanses me. Like I've been washed in holy water. It's a struggle to keep from staring. I don't remember half of the articles I've been pretending to read. When she laughs to herself at something in her magazine, it's a laugh that's so infectious that it touches your soul. Her walk is graceful and demure. It suggests that there could be no coffee shop without her presence. I've become captivated by this creature.

I've become accustomed to our weekends. Were it not for these Saturday mornings, the rest of my week would be a waste. What would I have to look forward to? I certainly wouldn't be at that coffee shop. Although the coffee is good, I come here for the "atmosphere". What would I do if that changed? I often find myself wondering if we ever get too old for crushes. Oh, how this distant infatuation has affected my whole life. And what's more than this, I don't know who she is. I don't know what she's about. I don't know what her interests are. I don't know her political stance. I don't know her favorite color. I don't know her dress size. I don't know if she's really noticed me, or if she just politely smiles at me to be kind. I know none of these things because I've never gotten the nerve to speak. The only thing that I do know is that she likes this coffee shop just as I do, and that she's beautiful beyond compare. Sometimes I kid myself into thinking that she's just as afraid to speak to me as I am to her. But let's be real. Surely that kind of beauty knows no fear. Right?

As I notice the time, I gather my things and prepare to leave. As the waitress arrives at my table to collect my bill, she catches me in deep thought about my dilemma. She also catches me mid-stare. As she thanks me for my tip and begins to walk away, she turns around and comes back to my table.

"Can I ask you a question?" she says.

"Sure", I said.

"Well, I've seen you come here every week for a while now, and I think you're pretty handsome. I know this is a bit forward, but I was wondering if you'd like to get together outside of this place and maybe get to know each other. What do you think?"

As I put my coat on, I took a look across that coffee shop at my infatuation.

"No thanks dear, I'm already taken", I responded with a smile. "But thanks anyway".

Just as I reached the door of the coffee shop, I looked back one last time. Just one last look to get me through the next six days. As I looked back, my brown eyed, brown skinned, freckled-faced angel caught my eye and smiled at me. A smile that seemed to say, "See you next Saturday".

My angel, I won't be late.

It's All About You

There's no real way to say or show how I feel about you. But I'll try. You are everything. You are everything that I have ever wanted. Everything that I have ever needed. When I'm with you, nothing else matters. The only thing that matters is that beautiful smile on your face. That look in your eyes. You move me in ways no one has ever moved me. Your touch is like magic. Your kiss is like heaven. To feel you next to me is like … it's like it was meant to be. When I wake up in the morning, you are the first thought on my mind. When I lay down to rest at night, you are the last thought on my mind. You are all thoughts in between. It's everything about you. You are my sun. You are my moon. You are my earth. Without you, there is nothing. With you, there is everything. I only wish that you could know the true depth of my love for you. It's very easy to feel, yet very hard to explain. But I know you feel me. Can't you?

Does your heart beat faster whenever I'm around, like mine does whenever you're around? Do you lose sleep when thoughts of me haunt you? In the middle of the night, do you crave me? In the middle of the day, do you crave me? Does the sound of my voice make you smile, no matter what? Do you wish that it were me every time the phone rang? Do you wish to spend every moment in my presence? Do you wish to hold me in your arms until the end of this life and the next? Please say yes. Say yes because these are all of the things that happen to me. These are all of the things that come with loving you. It's all about you. Everything from that beautiful smile to your deep, brown eyes to the curves of your body to your kissable lips to the smell of your perfume. It's all about you. I was made to love you. No matter what paths we may walk in life, you will always be in my heart. You will always be my heart. I kiss your hand to salute you. You are my queen. I could only hope to someday be your king. I would give you anything that your heart desires. My heart desires you. Does your heart desire me?

Say Yes

Across a crowded room she stands
My beautiful future
Champagne glass in her hand
As I plan my approach, I approach a plan
Do I perfect my game or approach her as a man?
The latter is the move
Gotta be a man about it
But be sure to be smooth
And yet, I'm stuck on pause
Paralyzed by the beauty this creature does possess
A guarantee is needed from you, my dear
Promise me you will …
Why is it so hard to find the words to say?
Doesn't this get easier with age?
I'm searching the mental dictionary
For the words that impress
For this angel walking among us
Both beautiful and blessed
For some reason, imagination refuses to take hold
Gimme a pen and some paper
And I promise I won't fold
You were always just a fantasy
And now we're here
My dreams have now been fulfilled
No longer fantasy, now you're real
I wanna approach, and yet I'm standing still
Scared as hell because I need something confirming what I feel
Promise me you will …
Wish I wasn't a ball of nerves
In the presence of your beautiful face
In awe of those magnificent curves
I'm swearing you're perfect
And we never even met
I'm believing your voice is angelic
And you ain't said a word yet
Every moment that passes, I'm holding my breath

Thanking God that another hasn't approached you yet
At that precise moment, our eyes have finally met
It's like heaven, a moment I'll never forget
And yet
My feet are in cement that's no longer wet
I gotta make this move
Or be forever filled with regret
But I need something from you
Promise me you will …
Say yes

Days Like This

Its days like this when I'm at my weakest. You know, when you're not here. When I can't hold you. When I can't smell your perfume. When I can't touch you. Some days are better than others. Sometimes, I can find something else to do. You know, something to take my mind off you. That lasts about 30 seconds to a minute. I thought of going to the doctor. You know, for therapy. But unless he's ever been in love with you, he would never understand. Sometimes, I wonder if the rest of the world can see that look on my face. That look of confusion. That's just one of the many emotions loving you can cause. What do I do? What do I say? Have I been calling too much/not enough? I've never understood how people in love can function in the world on a day to day basis. You know, without going crazy. What in the hell do they do to stay focused? The only thing I can figure is that they can function because even though they're in love, they're not in love with you. That makes all the difference in the world. Because if they were in love with you, sleeping at night would be something that they would only hope to do. And even when they did get that sleep, all they would do is dream about you. And when they're awake, all their thoughts would be of you.

All thoughts. And that's always a blessing and never a curse. I could only wish that you'd love me that way.

Do You?

KJ's Proposal

The re-evaluation is what I'm afraid of
Is it fame, is it pride, is it life, is it love?
Have I really put my focus where it needs to be?
Have I aligned myself with a path that sets me free?
Am I really seeking the warmth of a tender embrace?
Recognizing that heaven is in just one woman's grace?
Have I cleared out enough emotional space?
And freed my mind of all memories, save your beautiful face?
All I need is one woman to read my poetry
To be excited by my words as she flows with me
To share with me all the things life is showing me
To increase anticipation as she grows with me
Take my hand on this journey, come and go with me
I guarantee you'll be happy with what we come to be
Get deeper in my thoughts and I'll be deep in yours
Get deeper in my love and I'll get deeper in yours
Bring about a peace to my emotional wars
And when love is not enough, we'll give each other more
More than just a physical, be my spiritual wife
I'm not asking for now, I want forever
I'm asking you to save my life

Scene Three — Am I Losing You?

My favorite

An Open Letter from Aдam to Eve

Dear Eve,

It's all coming clear to me. I understand it now. I've been trying to figure out why we continue to be two, rather than one. I can tell you now. In fact, I will tell you. I will tell you in the next lines. It's my fault. It's your fault. It's our fault. There have been too many wrongs committed by me. I've failed you as a man. I haven't done what I was supposed to do. What I promised I would do. I promised to be faithful. I failed. I promised to respect. I failed. I promised to be a good father. I failed. All of these things I promised, and yet I never came through. Instead of showing you love, I pretended to be hard and acted as if I didn't care. Instead of being a father, I left you to raise the kids all alone. Instead of coming home at night, I went to bars and strip clubs. Instead of making love to you and only you, I slept with other women and put you at risk. My excuse? "I don't love her, but I love you and you should understand that". Somehow, that was supposed to keep you from hurting.

Instead of spending quality time with you and the kids, I chose to throw material things at the situation. Money, hairdos, jewelry, clothes and toys for the kids were supposed to take the place of an absent boyfriend, husband and father. To put it plainly, I treated you like a whore, and my kids like bastards. What kind of a role model am I for my son? What kind of man am I presenting to my daughter? Will she see this as normal, and go out and find a man just like me? Will she find a man that shows her love, respect and treats her like a lady, and dismiss him because she thinks he's "soft"? Will my son grow up and make babies, only to neglect them? Will he grow up and disrespect women in the way of his father? I don't know. The only thing I do know is that if I don't change, they'll be worse for it. But it's not all my fault. I'm not the only one to blame. You've failed as well. There are some things I need from you. Yes, you've failed too. The question is, how have you failed?

There have been too many wrongs committed by you. You've failed me as a woman. You haven't done what you were supposed to do. What you promised to do. You promised to be faithful. You failed. You promised respect. You failed. You promised to be a good mother. You failed. All of these things you promised, yet you never came through. Instead of raising the kids, you left them with grandma all of the time. Instead of staying home and being a good mother, you chose to run the streets with your girlfriends and party all night. Instead of making love to me and only me, you slept with other men and put me at risk, just to get revenge on me for my actions. Somehow, that was supposed to keep you from hurting over what I did. Somehow, that was supposed to hurt me and make me act right. Instead, it only continued a vicious cycle.

Instead of spending quality time with me and trying to work through our differences, you accepted material things from me instead. Money, hairdos, jewelry, clothes and toys for the kids were payment enough for you, instead of demanding that I be a better boyfriend, husband and father. To put it plainly, you acted like a whore, and allowed me to treat my kids like bastards. As long as you were living in a luxurious house and had lots of money to spend, it didn't matter to you what I did in the streets. Just bring home the paper. What kind of a role model are you for my daughter? What kind of woman are you presenting to my son? Will he see this as normal and think that the only way that he can gain the love of a woman is to buy it? Will my daughter grow up and become the same woman as you? Will she think that a man doesn't really love her if he's not emptying out his pockets for her? I don't know. The only thing that I do know is that if you don't change, they'll be worse for it. But it's not all your fault. You're not the only one to blame. We've both failed. There are some things we need to do individually, as well as together. But where do we start?

I can start by showing you the love and respect you deserve. I must learn to love you again. You should mean more to me than anything on this earth. I must return to a place in my mind where you are my life partner. Where I feel that I can't do without you. Because the reality is that I can't. I need you in my life. I can't let my pride interfere with that. I must be man enough to show you what you mean to me everyday. No matter what my friends say. I must return to a place where you mean more to me than just a place to lay my head.

You must become more to me than just a sexual conquest. You must become more to me than just the carrier of my children. You must become more to me than just someone that I take out my problems on, rather than talk out my problems with. I must return to a place in time when you were my Queen and I was you King. I must return to a place where I provided for you because I loved you, as opposed to giving you material things to cover up for my indiscretions and inadequacies. You should be my reason for living. Everything else should be secondary. I must regain my focus. One woman for one man. Two souls with one focus. To create heaven on earth for one another. I must return to that place. Again, the question is, what do I need from you?

If I prove myself worthy, you can start by showing me the respect that I deserve. You need to learn to love me again. I should mean more to you than anything on this earth. You must return to a place in your mind where I am your life partner. Where you feel that you can't do without me. Because the reality is that you can't. You need me in your life. You can't let your pride interfere with that. You must be woman enough to show me what I mean to you everyday. No matter what your friends say. You must return to a place where I am more than just a bank account to you. I must be more to you than just someone to put down to your friends when we have disagreements. You must return to a place in your mind where I am your man, and you are my woman.

You must return to a place in your mind where a man's bank account isn't the measure of the man. You must return to a place in your mind where you know the difference between a man who provides for you out of love, and a man who gives you whatever you want, just to keep you quiet while he sleeps around. You need to return to a place where it's not <u>as important</u> the size of the house you're living in, but rather with whom you're living. You need to return to a place where the size of your engagement ring doesn't matter <u>as much as</u> the character of the man that gave it to you. I should be your reason for living. Everything else should be secondary. You must regain your focus. One woman for one man. Two souls with one focus. To create heaven on earth for one another. You must return to that place. But we must do it together.

Since the beginning of time, we were meant to be together. From the moment God took one of my ribs and made you whole. So, after all this time, why have we decided to go away from one another? Why is there a great divide between us? I can tell you. There was a time when I had to adapt to your way of life in order to have you. It was that way because your way was, and still is, the best way. It's a way of peace. A way of love. A way of family. It's God's way. To adapt to my way of life would surely be self-destructive for you, and thus family as a whole. Unfortunately, that's where we are today. You have adapted to my way of life. And we have self-destructed. Instead of being my reward for turning away from my foul ways, you have become as promiscuous as I am. Instead of demanding that I respect you, you have allowed me to call you "bitch" and "ho" without reprimand.

You've only required that I increase your bankroll and your wardrobe in order to continue to behave in this manner. I have thus become more aggressive in my behavior. I show no remorse for the loss of your love. I've completely taken you for granted. You've taken what used to be a part of just being a man, which was taking care of his woman, and made it a license to abuse you. In turn, I've taught my seeds to disrespect the very womb from which they came. And you've allowed me to do it. Instead of condemning my whorish ways as you have in days past, you've chosen to wallow in this shame with me. Instead of leading me into the light, you've followed me into the darkness. But our fate has not been sealed yet. We can still be saved.

If you could turn your eyes from the dollar, and view love as the ultimate gift. If I could turn my eyes from my carnal desires, alcohol and drugs, and view love as the ultimate high. Because love is the ultimate. It's the greatest emotion that God has enabled us to feel. And we've turned away from it. But we can be saved. Because our Creator is still alive, we can be saved. We just have to be willing to work. We must work with renewed faith. We must rededicate ourselves. The Garden of Eden should have been the last time we went against God's wishes. But it wasn't. Surely you and I as adversaries is not what He envisioned when He placed us in the paradise that we eventually ruined. Let's create a new paradise. Let's return to the thrones from which we have fallen. You are my Queen. And I am your King.

Adam

All I Wanted ...

I never wanted what I saw on the TV screen
The world's definition of beauty
Though most didn't compare to you
Didn't need you at my beck and call
Just wanted your attention sometimes
Unlike the other men you dated, you were never just a flower in my garden
You were the ultimate rose
Putting all others to shame
I never wanted to interrupt your life
Just wanted to hear your voice each day
Didn't mean to be obsessive about our love
But my desire for you was strong
The pursuit of you was the pursuit of happiness
Never meant to push you away
To me, you were the ultimate high
Didn't mean to drown you in expectation
Never realizing that I didn't meet yours
I just wanted us to last forever
Just wanted what I saw within my heart
That we should always be together
All I ever wanted was to see your face each morning
To kiss your lips goodnight
To feel you near me
To inspire you as you've inspired me
To love
To madness
To joy
To sadness
To hold you in my arms
To see my children growing inside of you
To be the man that you always wanted
'Cause all I ever wanted was
You

Some things just aren't meant to be ...

Imagine How It Feels

Imagine how it feels when you first fall in love.
The fisrt look. The first kiss. Those butterflies.
It's magic. Almost heavenly.
Imagine how it feels the first time you miss hearing her voice.
Feeling her touch. Smelling her scent.
It's torture. Almost hell.
Imagine how it feels to anticipate her presence.
The waiting. The wanting. The needing.
It troubles you. Almost despair.
Imagine how it feels when euphoria is wearing off
The distance. The lack of phone calls.
It's terrifying. Almost maddening
Now, imagine how it feels to be losing her.
Your fears. Your tears.
It's sickening. Almost critical condition.
Wait, imagine how it feels when she's walking away.
The heartbreak. The heartache.
It's killing you. It's oh so deadly.
Man, imagine how it feels when it seems she loves him better.
Those feelings of betrayal. Because to her, you've been so good.
It's cruel. Almost insufferable.
Then, imagine how it feels when it seems she just don't care.
Your world upside down. It's a problem all your own.
Vital signs fading fast.
Imagine how it feels to know that, to her, you're just a memory
Sometimes good. Sometimes bad. But definitely in the past.
It's hopeless. Utterly hopeless.
Imagine, just imagine wanting to see her smile again.
To hear her laugh. To look in her eyes.
But it all seems like forever.
Just imagine what it feels like to want to live again.
To walk again. To breathe again. But she won't return to you.
Just imagine.
Imagine how it feels.

A Prisoner's Wish

Before I let you go
Before I set you free
It's imperative that you come to know
How this love has affected me

I've given all that I can to you
Sometimes, I've given too much
But it doesn't really matter what I've given to you
For some reason, it wasn't enough

I've wondered what my life would be
Living without your kiss
I always felt it'd be the death of me
That I'd sink into the abyss

As I stand before you bearing my soul
I can sense that you just don't care
My emotions are spiraling out of control
I can feel it everywhere

You continue to be untrue to me
And my heart can't take no more
A prisoner's wish, you long to be free
You don't love me like before

All I ever wanted was to make you smile
Yet I failed at every try
All I ever wanted was to be worth your while
Yet instead, you caused me to cry

All I ever wanted was for this love to live
Instead, I watched it die
I've given to you all I have to give
Now I must take these wings and fly

Fly to the highest mountain top
Where God grants everlasting peace
Until all of the pain of this love just stops
And my mind is at everlasting ease

7 Pictures

I woke up this morning
And I was missing you
When it was just a week ago
That I woke up kissing you

We've become torn apart
By the actions of us two
Now I sit here holding in my hand
Seven pictures of you

The first was from the day we met
You brought sunshine with your smile
Still amazed that I ever got the digits
And that you thought I was worth your while

The second was from 10 minutes after
The first time we made love
It was the bomb, so every morning for the next two weeks
You were the only thing I was thinking of

The third was from the moment you realized
That you were falling in love with me
Yet I hadn't quite come to realize
What this love would come to be

So for that reason, I held back
Your love, I seemed to ignore
I guess that's why you look so disappointed in me
When I look at picture four

Picture five is my least favorite picture of all
It's the picture where I made you blue
That's when you found out just how uncommitted I was
When you found out I cheated on you

Picture six is what I call the picture of pain
And it's a pain that has no end
In this picture you're in the arms of another man
This is the picture where you sought revenge

When I look at picture number seven I see
A woman that just couldn't take anymore
That's when you looked at me and said you were leaving
That's when you walked out of my heart's door

As I sit here on the edge of this bed
And my eyes well up with tears
It breaks my heart to think that it's all my fault
That I no longer have you near

It's a shame that you had to walk away
Before I realized I loved you true
And I'd give anything I have right now
To take an eighth picture with you

Just Like A Sunset

Just like a sunset, suddenly you were gone from my life. I don't quite understand why the paths in our lives crossed, but I know that I'm better for it. Though you never quite understood it, you meant more to me that you'll ever know. To look into your eyes was to somehow gain a true understanding of God's vision when He decided what beauty would be. To be touched by you was pure heaven. To kiss your lips is like no feeling I've ever experienced. Not a day has gone by since the first kiss that I haven't longed for more. My only wish was to hold you in my arms until the end of time. But it seems that separation was a must for you and I. I wished that somehow you felt what I was feeling. But I can't help but fear that you didn't. Something in me tells me that if you did, you'd still be in my arms. Instead, just like a sunset, suddenly you were gone from my life.

My days are much longer without you. My nights are increasingly sleepless. My heart is now an empty place. No longer full of hope, but instead full of wonder. My light in darkness has gone. The smile on my face is missing. The butterflies in my stomach are no more. I feel that I've lost a part of my soul. You were the difference in my life. The difference between sadness and true bliss. You were my proof of life. I knew I was alive whenever I was with you. Through you, I knew of God's grace. Only His grace could allow me to experience such beauty. Though my torch for you will eventually be extinguished, I'll never forget the way you made me feel. My eyes have never been so bright. My soul has never felt so free. My heart has never felt so full. My arms will forever miss you. You were the stars in my night, and my sun to start each day. But with every sunrise, there must be a sunset. And just like a sunset, suddenly you are gone from my life.

... I've Lost You Again ...

When I woke up this morning, I realized ...
... that I've lost you again
Yes, I still smell your scent in my pillows
See you face in my dreams
Hear your voice in my ears
Yet, and still ...
... I've lost you again
Gone is the sunshine of my days
The star in the sky of my night time
The same brown-eyed angel that stared up to me
As she lay on my chest after ... last night
So sad that I felt love, while you only felt the moment
My heart went too far with likes of you
By the time I realized you were only for a season, I had to face reality ...
... I've lost you again
Paranoia gets the best of me, as I swear you're with another man
Can't help but to think I was never enough
These insecurities you've nurtured and you never reassured
With actions, only with words
Each lie more painful than the last
Was he better than me every time you let him in?
Well, whatever ...
I've poured out my heart, but it was all in vain
Still, I realize ...
... I've lost you again
I wish I could lock you up, and throw away the key
But what good would it do?
You'd probably still forget about me
No longer the love of you life
Simply the jailor
No longer unrecognizable just in the heart
But also the mind
It's true, good love is hard to find
Everytime you leave my door
I wonder if it's the last time
I wanna beg you to come back

But I fear it would be in vain
It's clearer today than it was yesterday …
… I've lost you again

The Destruction Of Us

How do I begin …

I can start with the day I met you
I can still see it so clear
My heart would not allow me to stop
Until I had you near

You broke down every barrier
You changed my point of view
You broke every rule I had
You were all I wanted to do

But now our path has changed
The honeymoon is done
These days, we exist as two
No longer walking as one

Now every word I speak
Is like a dagger in your heart
And my every attempt at kindness
Pushes us further apart

As the storm clouds continue to gather
I must run for cover
'Cause I can't stop the rain or my tears
And I can't tell one from the other

You used to be my sunshine
The calm to all my fears
Now the sound of your voice when we're making love
Damn near brings me to tears

'Cause I can't seem to shake the image
Of another man touching you there
Another man kissing what used to be mine
Another man's fingers in your hair

When all your expectations
I somehow fail to meet
When all that I've tried to build for us
Lay in pieces at my feet

My daytime has turned to night
The light in my life is dim
'Cause every time I don't see you
I know you're somewhere with him

Your touch has now grown cold
Distance between us has grown
Even when we're together
I still feel all alone

And all I ever wanted
Was to somehow make you feel
The love I feel inside for you
A love I can't conceal

It was written all over my face
It would flow like blood in my veins
But now this pain will eat at my soul
'Til nothing else remains

The thing that hurts the most
As we crumble in despair
Is the lack of concern you show
The fact that you don't care

I'll drown in this sea of confusion
You've turned my joy to blue
And I'm starting to hate myself
For still wanting to be with you

The Trouble with Acceptance (Still Letting Go)

As I wake to the dawning of a brand new day
I once again ask the Lord if He would light my way
Heavy on my mind are thoughts of you and I
As I continue to converse with myself, I ask, why ask why?
She's gone from your life now so it's time you let her be
But the memories of what we once had are constantly calling me
But I must see past this selfishness that still resides in my heart
That makes me long for us to be together when I know we belong apart
We started as a spark and then we turned to flames
But now the fire that burns within me is no longer quite the same
And from the fire our love has burned to the ground like a ghetto 2-family flat
And though I know I'll rise from the ashes like a phoenix, it's you and I that I
can't bring back

When

When? Is the question she always asks
When will we embrace the future
And cease living in the past?
Placing her heart in my hands
As I shatter it like glass
When is the question that hangs in the balance. As she sits there patiently waiting. Her nails tapping the table, her eyes racing as fast as her heart beats. She doesn't want to hear me sing the same old tune. She knows my song, she knows my rhythm. She doesn't want to hear my story again. She's read every page in my book. She knows how my story ends.
When? Is the answer I must give
Indeed, the impatience has grown
I must act now or lose my inspiration
The intensity grows with each question
Where were you?
Where are you?
Who is she?
And what is she to you?
When?
When will the lies end?
When will true love begin?
Staring at me, the tears begin to flow from her eyes. Proof that what she doesn't know can hurt her. All she ever wanted was a good man. All I ever wanted was to conquer all that I see. Girls who flirt in tight skirts. Disregarding my princess that sits alone on the throne.
Waiting
Wishing
Wondering
When?
When will her prince come home?
When? Is the question
But I have yet to give an answer …

Fair-weather Love

We dance the dance of the sinful man
We unknowingly walk his path
Just out of the reach of the Father's hand
We enable this misery to last

My sanity is compromised from day to day
As I yearn to be in your good graces
I wander from soul to soul, seeking to replace you
With unfamiliar faces

Yet I can't erase us from my past
We're forever like clouds in the sky
In order to overcome and be born again
I must embrace you and I

I'm trapped in a prison I built myself
I've become a prisoner of me
I must bring myself to let you go
If I'm really to be set free

Your fair-weather love has infected my soul
And disrupted the system of things
Your love is like poison that destroys the body
And mortality is all you bring

And I can't deny what we were in the past
It's as real as the Father's love
A misstep in the journey of a young man's life
Is all it ever was

I've attempted to see the mountain top
But the climb was just too steep
I've attempted to erase you from all my dreams
Yet, still I get no sleep

Another change of weather should set things right
And once again your love will cease
Maybe this go 'round we'll be done for good
And my heart can rest in peace

Attention

Can I borrow your attention?
This expression of love simply can't wait any longer
It's what I've tried to deny
Yet, it continues to get stronger and stronger

For every moment that my soul seems to be dying
You have brought it back to life
Yet, no matter how I try to exist in your warmth
You treat me cold as ice

Yes, I have forgiven you
My heart wouldn't have it any other way
But it's all in an effort to have you back
'Cause this pain won't go away

My eyes aren't the same when they don't see you
They go from brown to blue
My hands aren't the same when they don't feel you
Now your lies are starting to sound true

Maybe he was only a friend to you
Paranoia was always my curse
I'm starting to learn to sing your songs
Though I don't understand your verse

Maybe you didn't get all of my messages
Technology's fooled me again
Just like my mind does when I walk away
Pretending we can just be friends

But it's my heart that begs for attention from you
It's my heart that misses you so
But my heart's unstable, so my mind is saying
It's time I let you go

Wish

I wish I could turn back the hands of time
To the day you and I first met
There are so many things I remember about that day
So many things I'll never forget

I remember the fist time I saw your face
An angel you seemed to be
But I would've never believed that an angel could bring
This constant pain to me

Wish I could've change my approach to us
Wish I had saw it for what it was
Now in so many ways I'm filled with regret
Wondering just what I was thinking of

Wish you could've appreciated the fact
That my love for you has no end
Wish I wouldn't have been so blind
When you said he was just a friend

Wish I had been much stronger in mind
When my thoughts you sought to rearrange
Wish I had been more realistic about who you were
And realized that you'd never change

Wish I could've saw the future in a crystal ball
And saw that you would be
As neglectful as you could be about our love
And show no real respect to me

Wish I wasn't feeling this pain that I feel
I should've allowed you to be free
Because I always knew you'd break my heart
Wish I had taken better care of me

Instead of always being concerned about you
And making sure that you knew that I cared
While you constantly left me all alone
Just wishing that you were there

I can't help but think that this pain was caused
By what I've put into the atmosphere
And now the smile that used to bring me joy
Is the same one that brings me to tears

The only thing more dizzying than the way we rise
Is sometimes the way we fall
Because now all I do is remember things
That I wish I couldn't remember at all

This pain has grown beyond my control
It's a pain I can no longer conceal
I wish that I had not been so blind to you
I wish I had known you weren't real

I wish I could be smarter about love
And take better care of my heart
Instead of turning it over to the likes of you
So you can tear it all apart

I've wished upon a thousand stars
Most times, I wished for you
I wished for us to be together forever
But those are wishes that will never come true

I think back to all those nights I wished
That you wouldn't hurt me like you do
But I have to stop wishing and make things happen
I have to let go of you

Last Night I Cried Again

It's happening to me all over again
Like it has so many times before
And I'm counting the times that I've lied to myself
Saying I wouldn't cry over you anymore

Yet I continue to be your voodoo doll
Taking the pain of your emotional pins
No matter what I do to try to make things right
With you, I'll never win

It seems that my prayers have gone unanswered
My unhappiness knows no end
My face is wet with the tears you bring
Last night I cried again

The reason I cried is familiar to me
It's a reason I know too well
It's the fact that no matter how much you say you love me
I never can seem to tell

A carousel of heartache
Is all that we've come to be
And no matter how many times you apologize
It all seems the same to me

I've done all that I could possibly do
To make this where you want to be
But no matter how much I try to show my love
I can't wish you right for me

The pain you continue to bring to me
Has become too commonplace
So much that we've both become unaffected
By the sadness in my face

It's just another day to you
But it cannot be to me
I can't allow myself to continue to be blinded
By the things you refuse to see

On Sunday my life was filled with "I love you"
By Friday you just didn't care
Now each night I drench my pillow with tears
When I reach out and you're not there

The pain that exists inside of me
Is impossible to hide
Yet the commitment you need to make things better between us
Either you can't or won't provide

Your disregard for us has touched a chord in me
I feel it everywhere
Though our love remains in a state of emergency
You ignore that as if you don't care

Your mind seems to remain in another place
You have more important things to do
You worry about all other aspects of your life
But the story of us isn't priority to you

You've taken my desire to remain in this place
For this, I'm not willing to fight
My heart is no longer safe with you
You're not willing to treat me right

My nights are filled with the pain you cause
That seemingly has no end
And my heart just breaks at the thought of you
Last night I cried again

Rejection Letter

The heart is never safe
In the hands of the likes of you
I should've been more careful with mine
I walked through your garden, eyes wide shut
Never realizing that your flower had been picked
Assuming I'd been the difference maker
Your mind regulator
Your soul embracer
Your body emancipator
Little did I know, you'd be my heart breaker
Brain devastator
Appetite disintegrator
Yeah, counterfeit ain't real, but you're way faker
Thought I could be your man
But I guess you showed me
Not quite qualified for the job
Check the mail, my rejection letter should be here soon
Never knew I didn't measure up to you
Should've let me know before I took the fall
Should've let me know before you locked me in prison walls
Took my time building a bed
Where you and I could lay
Never in my wildest dreams did I think so many
Would stay where I've stayed
Lay where I've laid
Play where I played
Should there ever been room in your bath
For a 3rd and 4th toothbrush?
Now I've fallen out of favor 'cause I asked for respect
Be careful what you ask for, because sometimes it's what you get
Wishing her away won't erase the pain
Trying to purify my thoughts
Won't remove the stain
Its just more time alone in my room
With this pen and this pad
Reminiscing on the worst experience

That I've ever had
You're no good for me, but somehow I'm good for you
Life's funny sometimes
Life's hard sometimes
Life sucks sometimes
Pick up the pieces of your pride
Go ahead and let her go
Make your way to the bus stop out in front
Of the Heartbreak Hotel
Another one will be along soon …

Some Sistas ... Some Brothas ...

Some sistas are every woman. Anything you need, you can find within her. A mother, a lover and a friend. But some sistas aren't women at all. They stay home all day, collect that check, and figure out ways to steal a good sista's man. Some sistas just ain't right. Now, some sistas are independent. They don't need a man to take care of or to take care of them. Some sistas don't need a man at all. But then again, every sista wants to be held sometimes. Now, some sistas hate the independent sista. The independent sista does nothing but point out that particular sista's shortcomings. Points out that she could be doing so much more with herself, rather than wait for a brotha to take care of her. But let's be real. Some brothas hate the independent sista, too. Some brothas feel that she's taking away his manhood. Some brothas can be a trip.

Some sistas are dedicated. To her family and to the role of wife. Even though some brothas don't deserve that, some sistas are just good that way. But other sistas are lacking. They're not dedicated to anything but the dollar. "No romance without finance" is what you'll hear them say from time to time. Some sistas don't know what life is supposed to be about. Those sistas will take just about anything off a man. Except lack of funds. Those sistas can't stay through the rough times, even if they can see that some brothas be trying. Now, some sistas will cook every night for her man. Make sure his food is hot and waiting for him when he gets home. Problem is, some brothas just can't bring their asses home on time. Some brothas can't stop running the streets. Some sistas are throwing themselves at these brothas. That's what keeps some brothas from doing what's right. Even though he's got a better sista at home, he can't stay away from that whorish sista. That sista does things that some other sistas just won't do. That whorish sista will pretend to understand a brotha, even though she don't care nothing about him. She could never understand him like that sista at home does. All this sista cares about is his bottom line. But still, some brothas will spend time and money on a sista like this, when he's got something so much better at home. Some brothas continue these trifling ways, while some sistas are at home, wondering when enough is enough.

Now, some brothas will try to fool a sista. They'll try to make a sista believe that everything is straight, when a brotha knows he ain't right. He'll try to make a sista believe that he's a good brotha, when he's not. Some brothas just don't deserve some sistas. Some brothas just aren't paying attention. They just don't know what they're putting these sistas through. Sometimes, they don't care. But some sistas are just plain tired. Some sistas are tired of washing a brotha's clothes and finding another sista's number in his pocket. Tired of cooking dinner for a brotha that comes home when he feels like it. Tired of a brotha's cell phone going off at 3am. Tired of a brotha leaving the room to have telephone conversations. Some sistas are tired of hugging what is supposed to be her man, and smelling another sista's perfume. Some sistas are tired of a brotha's excuses. Tired of a brotha's long, lost female "cousins" that he just ran into at the club, even though a sista ain't never heard him mention that name before. A sista's like, "Damn, what's up with that? She wasn't at the family reunion." Yet some brothas still don't get it. Just don't get it. But then a brotha wanna flip when a sista's checkin' out that brotha over there. And she will eventually check that other brotha out. Now a brotha wanna be jealous. Shame on you, my brotha. Ya'll just don't understand that some sistas are just fed up. Get yo' house in order, my brotha.

Life Has Finally Caught Up With Me

Life has finally caught up with me
And has shown me all of the pain I've caused some to see
So many years, sowing seeds of discourse
The mistreatment of many and showing no remorse
I had many opportunities, but never changed my course
Even though I knew payback would hit with much force
I did my lover wrong and all she did was love me more
And I traded all that in for meaningless intercourse
I hoped to get away but I knew it wouldn't be
For I soon found you and you eventually found me
All the wrong I've done in life has come crashing down on me
The dissolution of our love has brought about a change in me
Yes, the mistake of you and I is more than just streaming down my face
It's more than a feeling that's just commonplace
You were always part of the divine plan
A creation of the Father's hand
You were a sign of things to come
My best laid plans about to come undone
A vision of Karma brought to life
A pain so intense that it cuts like a knife
Captured, only to beg to be free
My life has finally caught up with me
So many broken hearts litter my past
Promises broken, commitments half-assed
Yet, I continued on, but not ignorant in the way
I knew I'd meet you someday
In the hour of the darkest midnight, I sought the light
Yet, I continued to make wrong out of right
Praying that my soul would one day take flight
Praying that Karma's force won't swing with great might
Knowing one day that you'd be here
Delivering revenge's promise both swift and severe
A manifestation of all the wrong done in my life
All the misery, heartbreak, pain and strife
And I waited, and waited, and waited
Hoping that you'd change your mind

And I hated, and hated, and hated
Knowing one day, it's me you'd find
And when I saw your face, I swear I heard the angels sing
A representation of heaven, for sure, but is it heaven or Karma you bring?
And I prayed and prayed that you wouldn't be
The manifestation of my life crashing down on me
A punishment for all the wrong I've done
My mistreatment of women who swore I was the one
You grew to be a flower that I should have known
From an impure garden of the seeds I've sown
You're a representation of the things that I've taught
How to be untrue pretending you'll never get caught
This experience is a teacher that one will never forget
Although my lesson is filled with pain, it's one I'll never regret
I must re-evaluate my relationships and tear down the garden of iniquity
And place my efforts into a woman that will grow with me
I must replant my seeds, but this time in fertile ground
So I'll no longer be weakened by your touch or sound
Re-order my steps so I'll no longer see
My life crashing down all around me

Fellas, be careful what you sew ...

When I Think …

When I think of all the things that you've said to me
Can't help but wonder what the truth should be
When I think of all the pain in my life you've caused
All the tears unforced from my eyes that fall
The brilliant performances you give, I applaud
All the times I wanna stand, but you force me to fall
How I try to force myself to give much less than all
And keep my knees from being scuffed as I'm forced to crawl
When I think of the many, many bad dreams you brought
When it was only love and happiness that I sought
It devastates me to the core to see that you ain't real
Just a pitch black soul with some sex appeal
Not being disrespectful, that's just how I feel
You'll see it one day in the Karma that'll force you to kneel
When I think about the opportunities I let go by
Sittin' around convincing myself that you were way too fly
To ever let you slip from my weakening grasp
Never knowing you couldn't see me, you just looked right past
It's such a shame we fall in love with the least deserving
And wind up doing things that are so disturbing
Like coming to your house in the pouring rain
And wishing you'd come out, but it's all in vain
Like hating your new boyfriend 'cause I'm not him
And wishing that he'd dog you like he did the rest of them
When I think about the changes you brought about in me
I know I should be glad that you set me free
You brought a darkness to my world that has engulfed my soul
To the point where my hatred is out of control
But when I think of all the heartache and the pain I've known
I take comfort in the fact that you'll reap what you've sewn

September

You're like a song that plays
Over and over in my head
And as I try to block it out
I simply sing along instead

Sometimes I catch myself thinking
That you and I have more songs to write
But then reality sets in 'cause I'm kidding myself
You no longer want me in your life

If you wanna try and forget me
Well, that's cool
If you wanna say you regret me
Well, that's cool too

If you wanna make yourself believe
That he can love you better
Then I guess I'll take what's coming to me
And you can forget I wrote this letter

But I'll never forget the smiles you gave
I'll never forget your laugh
I'll never forget the love we shared
I'll never regret our past

Like Whitney in her hey day
Didn't we almost have it all?
Now September is upon me, and I'm once again without you
Is it supposed to be this cold in Fall?

Our rendezvous was a desperate attempt
To somehow reach our dreams
But in a fit of selfishness we destroyed each other
Or at least to me that's what it seems

I may be confused 'cause I didn't understand your math
And I stayed up and studied all night
You took 3 days and made it greater than 4 ½ years
Somehow it just don't seem right

Maybe it all adds up and I just don't see
Maybe the answer's in the skies above
'Cause it seems you kept walking and you didn't miss a beat
I don't think that you'll miss my love

Now you walk with him and I walk with her
Again, it just don't seem right
Because my anger could've never matched the love I feel for you
And maybe that's why I can't sleep nights

So in the middle of the night inspiration came
And brought these words to me
I'm one natural disaster away from never speaking again
And I couldn't just let it be

Even though that's the way that I'm sure you want it
And this last wish I hope to grant you
But as you walk away again you must understand
My love was always true

Though we've come back together a thousand times
I get the sense this time is for real
I just hold on to the memory I have of the last time we kissed
In your eyes, your love was revealed

And I'll never forget that day as I held you in my arms
It was brief but it felt so right
And I'll remember the good ways in which you touched my life
And when I look to the skies at night …

… I'll think …

... Sometimes we hold on to the pettiest things
And allow pride to take us too far
So hopefully you're still reading as I write these final words
You'll always be my star

Dec. 31ˢᵗ

364 days and too many years to count.
End of days, end of year

What do I do, what do I do
When faced with the inevitable decision of you?

My emotional closet is filled with many memories of you and I. A fair chance at happiness is what we wanted. I thought I gave you the best chance. My math isn't as good as it used to be, but I think my calculations are correct.

Forgive me if I float in and out of rhyme and poetry
But I tried to take your hand and have you grow with me

Rejected again
Hmmmm

What do I do, what do I do
When faced with the inevitable decision of you?
It's time we move on from the days of you and I

No more kisses, no more hugs
No more getting high on emotional drugs
I worked so hard 'til there was sweat from my brow
We started out so happy, but look at us now
Put a gun to the head of this relationship
Pull the trigger and kill it dead
All I wanted was love and happiness
And I wound up with you instead

No disrespect in those last lines. And I'll hold no grudges for the lies you told. I'm no longer angry about the lonely nights. No longer pissed about the booty calls received before, during and after we made love. Can't be holding on to things that eat away at the soul. Check it out …

Keep holding on to grudges just like you're holding your breath
Soon you'll beg to let 'em go as you come face to face with death

No matter how you treated me, I gotta keep my life in motion
I put the memories in a treasure chest and I'll throw it in the ocean
Tears from my emotional eyes, the same ones you kept black and blueing
Made me realize these lies must subside, I'll let you go and keep on moving

I was surprised to find that you were better than me. Imagine that.
Thought you were looking down to me to lift me up,
But you were just looking down on me.
You weren't dying to be in my arms forever
You were dying to be set free
No more cutting me down with exact precision
No more sex to cloud my vision
It's 11:45 pm on New Year's Eve. 15 minutes to let you go. And in a way, it kinda hurts.

Gotta do what I gotta do and I'll miss you for a couple of weeks
My heart will probably beat a little faster everytime your name someone speaks
It's time to give in to my logical side, from your hands I shall be delivered
Although I'm afraid you'll call at 12:01 and my heart will reconsider
Hope all the new dudes work out for you, to you, I hope they're true
But in the event you wind up reaping what you've sewn
Call me
I'll tell you what I did when I was in your shoes

Footprints In The Sand

It doesn't really seem that long ago
You and I walked hand in hand
Before long, I carried you in my arms
And your footprints disappeared from the sand

As we walked along the beach of life
I sought to prepare you each day
For all of the valleys that come with love
And for the tidal waves coming our way

There were times when you hung on my every word
And listened to all that I'd say
But you never quite believed when I said to you
That someday you'd be walking away

Not because you didn't care for me
I know that the love was there
But the demons of the past kept haunting us
I could feel it in the air

You wouldn't accept the fact that things had changed
We grew further apart each day
Yet somehow you expected things to stay the same
When we both kept walking away

You put distance between us and we never recovered
You didn't realize the finality it'd bring
Sometimes absence makes the heart grow fonder
And sometimes it ends everything

There were so many things we shared together
Things special to you and me
But soon those things no longer seemed special to you
And I sensed that you longed to be free

There were times when I sat at the top of your list
For me, there was nothing you wouldn't do
But slowly it became apparent to me
That I was no longer priority to you

Before long you sought your independence
But with that there comes a price
It takes a lot to stand all alone, on your own
And start following your own advice

And as you pulled away, I was disappointed
But to yourself, you continued to be true
It wasn't until I accepted your brand new path
That it seemed to be affecting you

You seemed alright when you pushed me aside
And you seemed to be in control
But once you began to see the consequences of your actions
You didn't seem to be so bold

You didn't seem to take notice of what was going on
Until it seemed I was letting you go
Then it seemed that I had your attention again
And you still wanted love to grow

But you seemed to forget that I have feelings too
And they're affected by what you do
You forgot that I'm human and I've got my pride
And if neglected, I'll walk away too

But maybe it's too late to save this thing
Maybe the time to let go is at hand
'Cause when I look at our path, once again I see
Two sets of footprints in the sand

Maybe I've carried you as far as I can
Maybe it's time you go it alone
Or maybe it's time for someone else
To carry you all the way home

Swan Song

So many times I've played this role
So many times I've stood on this stage
So many times I've read this book of yours
But now I must turn the page

The performance I've given is one of a lifetime
In your mind, it will live on
But now the curtain's down, and the show is over
I give to you my Swan Song

I remember the last time I kissed your lips
Didn't know it would be the last time
It's a memory that will play forever and ever
In the corners of my mind

It's a gift and a curse the way I loved you
Sometimes, it just wasn't fair
You'd take my heart to the highest of highs
Only to leave me in despair

But like a Swan to a lake, I swam right through
All the rough waters of your love
And though I'm graceful in stature, I could never impress you
Quite like the flight of the dove

Yet he could never love you quite like I do
He never lived to brighten your day
Yet that never seems to be enough for you
So maybe it's time I sail away

Too many times we've said goodbye
And it always comes out wrong
So I'm no longer saying goodbye to you
I'm delivering my Swan Song

I sometimes felt you recognized
That the beauty of a Swan I possessed
But in reality I was no more than an ugly duckling
Someone you could easily forget

But don't get me wrong, this is not a sad song
Yet it's a performance I must give
As reluctant as I may be to concede
That together you and I can't live

See, I'm a warm weather bird and I take it slow
At least that's the story I've told
But you feel more comfortable with the winter days
For some reason, you like to be cold

And I tried and tried to give you warmth
And you continued to embrace the wind
I tried and tried to be your savior
And you continued to embrace the sin

I've prepared for this day since the beginning of time
And soon I will be on
As a hush falls over a sympathetic crowd
I'm preparing my Swan Song

Yet it feels as if I'm preparing my soliloquy
That's how it feels when I pour out my heart
As if you tune a deaf ear to all that I say
And you applaud when the stage I depart

Yet it's me that you swear never loved you true
No matter how wide my wings I spread
Instead of drawing you to the comfort of my embrace
I see you walking away instead

But don't worry about me, as if you do
I'll soon find another home
Although there was a time where if I didn't have you
I would rather have been alone

But that day is over just like my performance
As you seek to improve on me
And I used to wonder if I could let you go
'Til I realized you were always free

'Cause whenever it seems I loved you better
It somehow came out wrong
And now goodbye is all that's left to say
I've delivered my Swan Song

I AM …

I AM the destination you're seeking
I AM your willingness to sacrifice
I AM the thunder that rolls before the rain that falls
On the grass that is your life

I sink deep into the soil of your soul
I AM causing you to grow
I AM the spiritual revelation you must come to understand
I AM the enlightenment you must know

I AM the reason the love you feel for me
Will never ever grow old
I AM the recipient of all your negative forces
And I've somehow turned them to gold

I AM the deepest river you'll ever swim
So be careful not to drown
I AM the reason your spirit can be uplifted
When everything is down

I AM the ruler of your every thought
Resistance is futile, you see
I AM the controller of your consciousness
You'll never be free from me

You've tried to conceal me in darkness
But like the sun through the clouds I burst
You've said that the magic has gone from me
But I'm still your heaven and earth

I make emotional cripples began to walk
I revive the spiritually dead
You'll never erase me from your memories
I'll forever be in your head

Your pride will eventually betray you
Stubbornness is for mules
You should've succumb to the power of my love
You should've played by all of my rules

I AM even the rage that you feel
When you can't get me off your mind
I AM even the peace you believe that you feel
While drowning me in your bottle of wine

As you stroll though the garden of life with him
Convincing yourself that he's true
I AM the moonlight shining down on both of your shoulders
I AM even the midnight blue

I AM the inner sun that rises each day
To make the flowers of your heart grow
I AM affecting the every aspects of your life
In ways you'll never know

I'll haunt your thoughts forever
It's a fact, you'll have to face it
You foolishly took the blue pill
You'll forever be trapped in my Matrix

I'll forever be on your mind
You'll be a half, but never a whole
My presence will be with you forever
Until I disconnect your soul

... then it wasn't real

If the love you feel for me can vanish in a day
... then it wasn't real
You took me to the highest of highs
Then you showed me the lowest of lows
And if the magic that we shared can be gone in an instant
... then it wasn't real
You slipped the noose of love around my neck
And then you tightened it with each lie
Your lips were devoid of honesty
And if you can place both he and I on the same pedestal
And still claim to have love for me
... then your love wasn't real
Is it possible to truly love two?
Maybe ...
Is it possible for two to truly have your heart?
I doubt it ...
Is it possible that you loved me like you said you did?
I wonder ...
But if it can dissipate with just a simple war of words between us
... then it wasn't real
You truly mesmerized me
I was blinded by your physical beauty
But beauty must be complete
And if I can't see your inner beauty
... then your beauty wasn't real
I must hide my heart away from you
Unlike Whitney, I wanna run *from* you
But my feet are wet with the cement of our intertwined lives
Yeah, I feel like I'm stuck with you
But I loved you like you should've been loved
And you didn't return the favor
You stole like a thief in the night
You gave my love to another
Never giving me a second thought
And if you can't love me back like a real woman should
... then you aren't real

And if I close my eyes and pretend long enough
… I can pretend you weren't real

Familiar to Me

My head's spinning out of control
It's all happening to me too fast
Don't want this flame to burn too bright
I wanna make this fire last

I know I've seen or heard this before
This is a place I know too well
Yet I'm full of emotions that I can't explain
Look in my face, it ain't hard to tell

There's something about the way you smile
Something that I've known before
Don't know if I should get too close to this
Don't know why I come back for more

You're familiar to me like the summers of youth
Like the smell of springtime rain
Like the high school crushes that I had on girls
Who never even knew my name

You're familiar like the touch of a woman I loved
Like the warmth I felt from her embrace
Like the disconnection we eventually felt from one another
Like the tears it brought to my face

You're familiar like the rhythm of my favorite song
I can sing you word for word
Like the sound of love's voice when it calls my name
The sweetest sound I've ever heard

You're familiar like the dreams that I have sometimes
Of holding my unborn daughter
Yet I wonder if I keep getting close to you
Will I soon be drowning in deep water

If you're supposed to be my future, I'll wait for the sign
And may we never be torn apart
I'll take the memories of my heartaches and bring them all back to you
And leave them at the door of your heart

Are you familiar because you remind me of
A love that was once brand new?
Are you familiar because you remind me of
One who turned my life to blue?

My apprehension is what makes me stay away
A river of doubt divides us for now
And though I know I must overcome my fear
I just don't quite know how

Maybe I'm just wishing that somehow your love
Will come down and wash away all my sins
And though you feel so familiar to me
I'm not ready to love you again

My Path/Your Path

Everytime I want to give you trust
It seems it's just no good
Everytime I'm driving down your highway
I drive much faster than I should

Everytime you walk away from me
I fall deeper into the hole
But it's something about the way you look at me
That captivates my soul

I wish there was some other way
To express my love for you
I wish I could give you the diamonds you crave
But they don't measure up to you

I wish I had the monetary skills
To take you to distant lands
I wish I had the financial depth
To place the riches of this world in your hands

But all I have to offer is me
And I guess that just won't do
You'd string me along your garden path
But you'd never love me true

Sometimes I don't know who you are
Or what you want to be
I know what I have to offer you
But I'm not sure you want to see

From a distance I can see what path you're on
And it'll all come crashing down
I can see that you don't know which way to go
In your mind, there's confusion abound

In this life, we were to remain on our thrones
Never to fall from grace
Knowing that royalty is more about majesty
And less about the paper chase

Your eyes are so full of the cash's green
That you can't tell me from him
And the fact that my love flows like the deepest of rivers
But now I see that you can't swim

I can't make you happy with the love I give
Only with the things that I buy
Even if on one hand I've financed your dreams
And on the other hand I've made you cry

You can't quite seem to accept the fact
That love is the ultimate high
Instead you hold on to shallow dreams
While on a bed of thorns you lie

But who knows, maybe my thoughts are unclear
Maybe superficiality isn't wrong
Maybe I should adapt to the changing times
Maybe my spiritual quest is wrong

Maybe the quest of a man that's trying to do right
Is a quest for the sad and alone
Maybe I should give up the thought of divinity
Maybe those days are long, long gone

Maybe it's my fault that the devil keeps hurting me
And that I'm constantly in love with the wrong girl
Maybe the road to my happiness
Is to adapt to the ways of the world

I'll start by disregarding the feelings of others
No matter how they feel about me
Then I can proceed by breaking their hearts
If they impede my need to be free

Then I should be about carnal desires
And changing women like it's not even funny
And only do for those that do for me
And constantly be all about money

Yes, I think I'm ready to do this
I'm ready to run with the crowd
I'm ready to show off the brand new me
I'm ready to shout it out loud

Yet, strangely enough, I'd still be appealing
To many, and not just a few
Yet, strangely enough, if I became all of this
I'd still wind up with you

So is it worth it to trade my soul
For all the riches and fame?
Is it worth it to give up the pursuit of righteousness
To be the ruler of this game?

I'd rather hold out for something better
If it takes all day and all night
I'd much rather stay the course that I'm on
I'd much rather do what's right

I'd much rather choose a path of light
Than one that's dark and dim
I'd much rather not conform to your ways
Ways that I've come to condemn

I'd much rather disappear from your life
And allow you to go your own way
If north is good for me, and south for you
The neither of us should stray

Yes, conforming to the ways of the world
Ain't quite what I'm thinking of
I'd rather hold out for what God has promised
I'd rather hold out for love

The Garden

From the beginning she displayed
All of her perfect imperfections
Yet somehow she still felt worthy
Of all my love, all my affection

I was tempted by her beauty
Tempted by God's design
Drawn to this youthful spirit
At the hands of love I became blind

With a smile she drew me out
With a touch this journey began
With a gentle kiss, I tasted her lips so sweet
But I couldn't taste the sin

With a sweet voice she called me out
In the Garden is where we would meet
As that same sweet voice began to speak to me
"I have something I want you to eat"

As I tasted the fruit of her tree
Her lips gently touched my cheek
I consumed the whole of her poisonous fruit
Never realizing it would burn so deep

The sickness consumed my body
But I ignored what I felt inside
I pretended to bask in the glow of love
Before I knew it, I had already died

As my body lay lifeless in the Garden
My spirit began to rise
On my way to meet my God
On earth, I would no longer lift my eyes

As I reached the gates of Heaven
Before I could see God's face
I met the most beautiful Angel
She placed both of her hands on my face

"I have a message from God", she said
"This is not where you belong
You shouldn't be here right now
Your timing couldn't be more wrong"

"Your journey here is premature
Your time has not yet come
You must return to the Garden
There's still more work to be done"

"He hasn't sent you to the Garden to fail
He hasn't sent you there to die
He never wanted you to suffer
He never wanted your eyes to cry"

"He sent you there to inspire
He sent you there to uplift
He sent you there to touch the hearts of men
He sent you to share your gift"

"But what of the woman He gave me?", I asked
"Because of her, I have come here
Because of the pain that I've suffered
Returning to the Garden causes me fear"

"Fear not, because God is with you", she said
"And your mission must be complete
It's not the woman that brought you here
But rather your wandering feet"

"You lost sight of God's plan for you
You lost sight of His vision
You must lean on God and not your own understanding
And resolve to complete your mission"

"You were meant to be a blessing to the woman
Love you were meant to reveal
But because she disobeyed the voice of God
Her fate has already been sealed"

"But you mustn't worry about her
The mission must be your only concern
You're not yet ready to enter the gates of Heaven
These wings you'll have to earn"

And before I could speak another word
She gently placed her hands on my eyes
"Now is the time for sleep, mere mortal
And when you awake, you'll be a little more wise"

As pain ran through my body
I felt all the poison release
As tears ran down my face
I fell into a deep sleep

When I opened my eyes again
I lay naked in the Garden
Feeling that I escaped the execution of hell
And praising God for the pardon

The woman was nowhere around
She was gone without a trace
I felt free from the pain she caused me
But I still selfishly missed her face

As I reflected on the Angel
I remembered the things she told me
I realized that I had lost my faith
The faith that God would hold me

I realized that I lost my focus
Lost sight of God's vision
And it was that lack of faith that caused me
To deviate from my mission

But I must remember that I'm flesh
And the flesh can sometimes be weak
And I was only trying to show love to another mortal
And that's why I ate from her tree

Poisoning me is just what she did
But was it part of the divine plan?
But I can't spend my life grieving for her
I must place it in God's hands

But one can't help but wonder
Could this pain have passed me by?
Why did I have to travel this road?
Why did I almost die?

But it was because of me
I suffered at my own hands
It was what I had to go through
This was also part of God's plan

As the Angel said, I'm wiser now
I understand God's expectations
I was never meant to suffer at her hands
This was part of my purification

And now my faith in God
Is reinforced, and therefore strong
And now I can see He never left me
He was protecting me all along

Love's Eulogy

Dearly beloved. Brothers and sisters. Members and friends. It is on this somber occasion that we come together to mourn the passing of a dear friend. Indeed, this passing was a shock to the very few that didn't know the departed. But for those unaware, this death was simply a matter of time. This love that was shared between me and the young lady in the black on the front row was bound for the coffin that lies before you.

Loved ones, you may come by for one final viewing of what she and I once shared. Take a look inside and you'll see all that we've lost. A kiss between lovers. A smile. A laugh. The dreams of a family. The love we made. Yes, all things beautiful in nature. But there are also the missed and ignored phone calls, the lack of affection, and the general disregard for the relationship here. The infidelities, indiscretions, the late night phone calls when she swears she didn't know why they were calling at 2am. All gone away, never to return. A sad occasion, indeed. But in so many ways, our love's time had come.

As I eulogize this love of ours, I want you all to know that we did the best we could to revive this love. But it simply wasn't to be. Sometimes the heart has given all that it can. Sometimes there's no sense in life support. Sometimes, you have to let go. It's always hard when you've watched it grow from its infancy. You saw it growing through those stages of adolescence. Our names were written on love's high school notebook. You-n-me. But as love continued to grow, we continued to grow apart. My forgiving nature tested each day. Her irresponsibility continuously on display. Like all of us, this love was destined for the cemetery.

Go on and cry. You got to let it out, lest the pain consume you whole. The moment is filled with sadness, but this is a day of rejoicing. She and I no longer have to pretend that love is still with us. It's been gone for quite some time. I hear the whispers amongst those of you in the congregation. "But they seemed so happy together". Yes, love appeared to be as healthy as you feel right now. But we're all sick enough to die, and love was no different. It just kept its sickness from you. 'Cause if you thought it could die, then you might not believe in it anymore. And though this particular love has died, like Christians, it can be born again. In the hearts of someone brand new. A young man full of hope. A wide eyed young lady with big dreams of happily ever after. Yes, don't let the death of our love take your hope into the ground with it. There's still time for you. Find a new love. Recommit yourself to the love you have now. Death is a sign of things to come. Change the way you're living or your love to will die, never to know eternal life.

As we near the end of our services, I'd like to ask her potential next lovers and my potential next lovers that are serving as pallbearers to come forward to carry our love to the hearse. Friends, family and well wishers, please stop by and give my ex-girl your condolences. She'll cry tears on your shoulder, but somehow, through those tears, I think she'll be alright. Don't ask me how I know that.

Intermission

Now it's time for a brief poetry break. Well, not completely, but you'll get the idea. I know you've all been smiling and crying and reminiscing over my poetry, but it's time to put the handkerchiefs and tissues away for just a little while. There's more to come, but I needed to give you all something else to read besides stories of love found and lost. As I was compiling some of the poems that I wanted to include in this project, there were some other things on my mind. Things related to my people, but also things that relate to all people in general. I don't know if I'll ever be able to write a book without including some sort of commentary on the things that I feel are important and noteworthy.

In this brief section, I'll cover some things that I've covered before, like the image of black America and what we as a people need to address. Also, we'll dip into relationships in a piece I wrote for my website, www.kjworldonline.com. Most importantly, I'll give a brief tribute to my family. There were a couple of pieces that I wrote for our family reunion in 2005 that a lot of people enjoyed, so I decided to publish them. I've lost a couple of aunts since my last book was published and I've included a poem that was read at both of their homegoing services. There are also a couple more pieces that I liked and decided to include in this section. I guess this would constitute the "spoken mind" section of the book. It is my hope that you're enjoying the poetry that you've read so far, but please allow me this brief detour so that I may salute my family and share a few thoughts on some issues rolling around inside my head. We'll be back to the poetry soon enough. Or better yet, "'Scenes From The Blue Book' will be back after these messages".

There's Nothing Like Family

There is nothing like family. Wait, let's begin again. There is nothing like the black family. No one loves like we do. No one prays like we do. No one argues like we do. No one forgives like we do. Eventually. No one gossips like we do. And, most of all, no one cooks like we do. Sure, there are many other families from many other races that probably feel the same way. But, I'm convinced that we love like no other race can love. Through thick and through thin, it's a love that will always remain. If you've ever been loved and embraced by a black family, it's a feeling that's truly like no other. Yes, it's true. Once you go black, you never go back.

I've often wondered why we love like we do. The only thing that I can figure is maybe it's because of all of the pain our people have endured over the years. From the time we were taken from our homeland and brought here to be slaves. From the time we were separated from our loved ones and sold off piece by piece. From the time we were given a token proclamation and so-called freedom. From the time we were forced to the back of buses and made to drink from separate and unsanitary drinking fountains. From the time our leaders were gunned down like animals. From the time we were hosed down in the streets for simply disagreeing with the way we were being treated. From the time we were drafted and sent off to war to fight for a country that didn't even love us. Somewhere during all of these injustices, we came to a conclusion: We all we got. We had to love each other because no one else did. It's that level of closeness and many, many nights in prayer that brought us from the cotton fields and dirt roads to where we are today.

Every two years, the Flowers-Jones-McFolley family comes together to celebrate. We celebrate our successes, celebrate the new additions to our families and we remember fondly those that have gone home. Officially, it's a family reunion. Sure, anybody can get together, throw on some ribs, get a hustle going and tell loud jokes that no one really seems to get because they weren't born when some of these things happened, but that's really no more than a picnic. It takes a real family to make it something more. But it's really a family celebration. You can look around the room and see how far we've come. In one form or another, every stage of our progression is represented here. In one sweep of the room we can celebrate all that we've come through in the past, and all that future holds for us. To those that have paved the way for us, we thank you and we will carry the torch and make you proud. For those of us that will be the torch bearers for this family, don't disrespect the cotton fields and dirt roads that I've mentioned. Those that traveled those roads made a better life for us through their sacrifices. Through more opportunities, we may have more education, but they have more wisdom. We may not see it in our fancy books of higher learning, but there is a difference between the two. As the saying goes, we're all living off of someone else's prayers.

Through the years God has kept this family. We couldn't have made it this far without Him, and we must remember that we need Him going forward. Though we come together physically every two years to celebrate, we should come together emotionally much more frequently. Though we're no longer right up the road from one another, technology has fixed it so we can reach out and touch each other with great ease. Some of us here haven't seen or spoken to one another in, well, two years. This year, when we exchange numbers, let's not just do it for show. I know sometimes we give a fake smile to Sister So-and-so on Sunday morning, but this should be different. This is family. Starting today, let's put that 20 year old argument to rest. For good. Look and around this room and appreciate your family. We all we got. There's nothing like my family.

Every Two Years

Every two years
We come together as one
To remember all that we've been through
And celebrate what we've become

Our youth is represented
As are those that paved the way
Those that taught us pride in the family name
Those that taught us how to pray

We reconnect with our loved ones
And tell stories of days gone by
We share inside jokes that only a family can share
And we laugh until we cry

We rejoice in the new additions that we may have
And welcome them with a warm embrace
And as far as anyone's eyes can see
It's hard to find an unhappy face

You see people that you haven't seen in years
You meet family that you've never known
You see children that you haven't seen since they were babies
And you marvel at how they've grown

In the eyes of the older generation
You can see all the places we've been
And you can see in our youth, our family's future is bright
And it's a future that has no end

We reminisce on those gone to be with the Lord
It may cause us to shed some tears
But we mustn't be sad, just remember the good times
Though we still wish they were here

As we hold hands in prayer before the family meal
We reflect on all that is good
And thank God that we've come together on one accord
Like a family that loves one another should

And when we finally come together on Sunday afternoon
We'll hug and say our goodbyes
Though this two year celebration has come to an end
Let's not let our love subside

As we return to our homes all over this land
And we're two years away once again
Let's hold on to all of the love that we shared
Until we meet again

For Aunt Maggie and Aunt Stella
On My Way Home

I've played my part in the Master's plan
Now my time has come to rest
I hear a voice in my head saying it's time to come home
To the One that loves me best

Some family and friends have gone before me
And they're waiting on the other side
Don't cry over the house where I used to live
Rest assured, I'm still alive

Though I'm no longer here in the physical sense
I haven't left you alone
But this is a journey I have to make
I'm finally on my way home

Don't allow the sadness to take away
From the joy we shared together
But the time has come for me to be
In the presence of God forever

There's a brand new life waiting for me
Just across the Jordan stream
I'll take my place in the Heavenly choir
And the praises of God I'll sing

When I finally make my way to the Kingdom of God
I'll shout hallelujah all day
'Cause there'll be no more pain and struggles for me
It'll all be taken away

There'll be nothing but joy and gladness there
No more reasons to say goodbye
There'll be no more heartache and sadness there
No more tears from my eyes

I'm on my way home from this earthly place
And I'm going home to stay
But don't worry about me, 'cause in my heart I know
We'll meet again someday

Resolution

This is my resolution. But this resolution isn't just for my New Year. This resolution is for my New Life. For so many times in our lives, we resolve to change for the new year. So many times we make resolutions, only to change shortly thereafter. For many years I have resolved not to resolve for the New Year. "What's the point?" I figured. "It will only be forgotten in the weeks to come." "Besides", I often wondered, "why does it have to be New Year's Day before I resolve to change?" But now I understand. In fact, I understand it fully. The new year represents something new. A new beginning. Starting over. As the new year starts, we should start over. Out with the old, and in with the new. It's not just a brand new day, it's a brand new year. As the calendar goes from the old year to the new, we should go from our old ways to new as well. This is my resolution. To go from the old ways, to the new.

There are many definitions for the word "new". Some of them include "never used before", "just discovered or learned", and "starting over again in a cycle". However, there are two that stand out from the others. Two that represent how I feel. "Changed for the better". "Rejuvenated". That's what I feel. That's how I must be. Changed for the better. Rejuvenated. As the new year comes, I must reevaluate my life. Take stock of what I am as a man, what I'm about to become and what I want to become. The Bible says that every branch within me that doesn't bear fruit, God takes it away from me. But every branch within me that does bear fruit, He purifies and makes free from sin, so that it may bring forth more fruit. So this has become my mission. My resolution. To become changed for the better. To become rejuvenated. To allow God to purify all that is within and around me that's bearing fruit, so that it might bear more fruit. To allow Him to remove all that is within and around me that doesn't bear fruit, for it will only contribute to my downfall. As the new day dawns, a new spirit must also dawn within me. As the new year is realized, a new man must come to the forefront. I realize now that every new year, as well as every new day, is another chance that God has given us for a new beginning. I won't let that chance pass me by again. This is not just a New Year's resolution. This is a New Life's resolution. Staring today, I am new. Just discovered or learned. Starting over again in a cycle. Rejuvenated. Changed for the better.

Tribute To The Black Mother

In times of desperation
She will always be there
When the world turns it's back on you
She always seems to care

She's the black mother
Proud and strong
Never yielding to take her place
As the family backbone

In a tidal wave of confusion
She'll always make perfect sense
When in the face of evil
She uses love as her defense

Forever protecting her children
From the devil's hands
When by your side there's no one else
Mother will always stand

No matter how wide the ocean
Or how deep the river seems
No matter what the consequences
No matter how extreme

She remains our only constant
The queen of all she surveys
And any love that is required
She gives without delay

So each and every day
We should give to her what's due
For every day should be Mother's Day
So every day our love is true

The Glass

Now, it's time to talk about something that men and women have been doing since the beginning of time. Cheating. Now, I'm not gonna break this thing down from beginning to end. What to do and how to get out of a situation where you're being cheated on and all that. If you want that, you can go out and purchase my first book *Temporarily Disconnected* (shameless plug). What I'm gonna talk about here is something I like to call "The Glass".

The Glass is something that we first learned about in an assembly at school, but as we got older, we begin to apply it to another aspect of our lives. When we were in Elementary, Jr. High and High School, we all had to go to that assembly in the auditorium on safety. One of the things we were taught about was the fire extinguisher that was encased in glass. Remember what that glass said? If you don't, here ya go: "In case of emergency, break glass." Sound advice, wouldn't you agree? Short of an available water hose, how else were we gonna put out that fire? Little did our local Fire Marshall Bill know, we would someday apply such wisdom to putting out our relationship fires. Whenever we have a supposedly out of control fire in our relationship, we break the glass. Only thing is, we don't have extinguishers in that glass, we have gasoline.

That gasoline exists in the form of another woman or another man. However, I call it gasoline because it doesn't put out the fire, it simply intensifies the flames. Now, for some of you, it does put out a certain fire, but as far as your relationship is concerned, it either takes a bad situation and makes it worse, or it takes a worse situation and ends it altogether. But what makes this unfortunate situation kinda funny is the different ways in which men and women handle it. Although there is no "right" in cheating, because by nature cheating is wrong, there is a sensible way to do things, and then there's a man's way. Allow me to explain.

Every woman has a man in that glass. Whether she's a single woman, a loose woman or a faithful woman in a committed relationship, she has that man somewhere. Since we're talking about relationships, let's focus on the faithful woman. This woman will only use this man in case of emergency. Now a faithful woman's relationship emergency is just that: An emergency! She won't break the glass because you wouldn't take the garbage out once or twice. She won't break the glass because you came home late once or twice. She won't break the glass because you said you would call back in 5 minutes and it's been 3 hours. She won't do it because you forgot it was Valentine's Day. No, she won't do it for something frivolous. She understands that this "tool" has to be used in the case of an actually emergency. There are no false alarms here. No pulling the fire alarm so that we can get out of class for 20 minutes.

If the faithful woman breaks that glass, there's a fire somewhere. But it's not just some small garbage can fire. It's a fire that's out of control. She's tried to fight it with a glass of water here and there, but it's apparent that won't do. It's time to come with something a little more substantial. In other words, she'll break that glass because you never take out the trash. She'll break it because you not only come home late all the time, sometimes you don't come home at all. It isn't broken because you have no sense of time when it comes to calling back when you said you would, it's broken because you never call. It's broken because you don't even know when Valentine's Day is or why it's special to her. That goes for anniversaries and birthdays as well. Yes, when a woman takes a hammer to that glass, we have truly gone too far.

But what about us and what we as men go through? What about when our women push us to break the glass? Well, a man's breaking the glass is a little different. It doesn't take as much to push us to "the edge". Interrupt us watching the game? We might have to go to the glass on ya. Complain too much? It might be time. If we have to ask twice for a sandwich? Better watch yo' step, girl. Oh, and here's the big one. Turn us down for sex, no matter the reason, time of day or night or what ever your medical or physical situation may be, and you can best believe that's grounds for glass breakage. We're very, very temperamental ladies, so you gotta watch your step.

Now, as I said before, anytime either of us goes to the glass, it's not a good look. When we go to the glass, that means there's a problem, and as I wrote in my first book, we have to talk our problems out, rather than act them out, because most times, our actions without talking produces an undesirable result. Believe it or not, this is something that's more beneficial to men more so than women. That's true because of what I stated earlier. Men go to the glass for no damn good reason. When women go to the glass, it's a last resort and they're at a breaking point. And they've usually put a lot of thought into it. Allow me to explain.

When a woman goes to that glass, she's picked out her candidate very carefully. She's done it so well, that most times, even her candidate doesn't know he's been chosen. Even though women can gossip like nobody's business, they actually know how to keep a secret when they really have to. She's usually picked out somebody that she can do what she wants to do with and no one will know. She already knows that she won't tell, and somehow, some way, she's figured out that he won't either. She's done her job so well, that she's 110% sure that when she makes her move, not only will he reciprocate, he'll even pay for the room (because unlike us, they're never stupid enough to bring it home or anywhere that her man comes frequently). She's already put out feelers to be sure of that. He's either on the job, in the neighborhood, or believe it or not, he may be a member of the congregation. Hell, you may even know the brotha personally. And you wanna know the kicker, fellas? Because I'm talking about intelligent and faithful women in this piece (as opposed to some young and dumb one that will spread her legs for any man that's willing to spend a dollar or two on her), 9 times out of 10, he's a better man than you. More romantic, more caring, better job, better educated, loves his mama and all that.

However, when we go to the glass, it ain't quite the same. In fact, we're so lacking that we don't even use the hammer that the woman uses. We break it with our hands, thus leaving a trail of blood to the other woman's house so that we can be tried and convicted later. My brothas, my brothas, what are we doing? Our "woman in the glass" is a far cry from the woman we have at home. Forgive me if this gets harsh ladies, but just like some of us are losers, some of you are as well. When we have a woman in that glass, she's usually a woman that nobody else wants for whatever reason. She's that woman that you call when you just left the club alone, nobody else is up or you can't call your girl because she'll know how late you were out when you actually told her you were going to bed. And besides, your penis has convinced you that going to bed without sex is a no go.

She's that woman that you'd never be seen with in public. You won't let her come to your house unless it's between 1 and 5am, and she must be gone before the sun comes up. The same applies when you go to her house, and you always park 2 blocks over in case somebody comes through and recognizes your ride. Her self esteem is just low enough for her to allow you to treat her this way, but somewhere in her mind she thinks that you think she's special because you brought her some Coney Island on the way over. And you wanna know the kicker, ladies? Because I'm talking about idiot men that don't know when they've got it good as opposed to a man that knows how to treat his woman, the woman he's cheating with ain't half the woman you are.

There are several morals to this piece here. A lot of us have that glass in our relationships. Some of us don't and if that's you, consider yourself lucky. But if you do, you must find a way to eliminate it. It may seem like a good idea, but it will always cause more trouble than it's worth. Unlike my first book, when I talked about the women having the most to gain in turning the relationships around, it would be most beneficial for men to correct this situation. Simply because women make better choices than we do in this situation. When we break the glass, it's usually because we're horny and can't control ourselves. Never make a decision when you're horny because there's only one answer to that question: sex! But once you're done, that otherwise undesirable woman is the broken glass lying at your feet. And when your woman finds out (and she will if she doesn't already know), you'll be stuck with her. When you get dumped, you'll visit her more often to satisfy your urges, thus creating the illusion of a relationship and now you're caught in a web so intricate that Spiderman would be impressed.

When you think about that man in the glass, he's everything that you could be, but won't be for whatever reason. Which means your woman is settling for less. Which means she must really love you to do so, despite all of your faults. Don't make her break that glass and go for the upgrade. All she wants you to do is step up as she has (if she has; I don't want all of you women that aren't taking care of your man inserting yourself into the role of "good woman" here). You don't always have to be Superman to impress your woman, you just have to be good to her. We've got a lot of women that aren't so bright that will go astray for the wrong brotha just like we will for the wrong woman sometimes, simply because he sold her a bill of goods about what he would do just to get in her underwear. They don't always realize that they don't need all of the things these dudes are promising. They just need somebody to treat 'em right. Everything else will take care of itself. So, the next time you and your woman have a disagreement, don't make her wanna break the glass. At the same time, you should avoid the glass as well. Instead, just go out, buy her some flowers and then take out the trash like she asked you.

Live From the Entertainment Industry: The Nigga Files

A question to all of my brothas and sistas out there: Is it time for the "bitches", "hos" and "niggas" to retire? And for that matter, the "hoochies", "chickenheads" and "'hood rats" as well (the "skeezer" has long since left us, although the "trick" has made a comeback)? As I get older, I find myself asking this question more and more, and recent events in the entertainment industry has put this question on blast in my mind. Yes, these words are considered offensive by many, but at the same time, they're used by just as many. But is there a place where these words, labels and accusations are acceptable? I wonder.

Hip hop artists have made careers from using these words and until recently, a lot of us, myself included, have just tuned a deaf ear to what we were hearing and hit the dance floor, shakin' our butts as if the words don't apply to us (although I'm not a part of the butt shakin'). But when Michael Richards, who played "Kramer" on the TV show *Seinfeld*, called us niggers from the stage of a comedy club, or when radio host Don Imus, whom I now call Imus The Terrible, calls our women "nappy headed hos", it's time to march, it's time to protest, it's time to boycott and it may even be time to fight.

When this type of thing happens in the entertainment industry, the first thing that happens is the publicists come out with their apologies and the spinners are so deadly that they'd put any car in the 'hood to shame. One of the many defenses put up by the white media and Hollywood is that a lot of this language was started, and has since been perpetuated in the black neighborhoods. A lot of this is in our beloved hip hop music. A lot of these things are true. But just because the hip hop artists and comedians of my generation sometimes disrespect women in the name of art, does that give any "artist" in the world that right? I don't think so.

"What up, my nigga?"

How many of us have used that greeting? If you're as closely related to hip hop as I am, you have. Some never heard it until Jackie Chan said it in the movie *Rush Hour*. Comedy. Very funny. However, even though it was funny, the reaction of those brothas in the bar in that particular scene was accurate. If anyone other than another black person said that to us, it's on. And in reality, Jackie would've never made it out of that bar without the assistance of a medical staff. Yes, in the words of the late, great James Brown, we don't know karate, but we know karaazzy. Some don't believe it, but we do use the word in that "greeting" as a term of endearment. To ask some of us to stop using the word "nigga" in our greeting is in some ways asking us to stop showing love. Sounds crazy, but it's true.

The flip side of this is that the word still stings for all of us, depending on who's delivering it. As I stated in the last paragraph, to say "What up, my nigga" to some of the boyz in the 'hood would generate a response of "Nothin', just chillin'". No outrage. No boycott. No offense. No fight. Just love. Just a greeting. But if someone from the south that heard that same thing from a white man many, many years ago with different connotations, i.e., "Hey nigger", it feels a little different. Coming from the mouth of a white person, it's less a question about how you're doing, and more a statement about how they see you and how they feel about you. When some of these words are spoken by one black person to another, whether you believe, accept or approve of it or not, it can mean a myriad of things. Love, hate or whatever. But when a white person says it to a person of color, there's no question or doubt about it. You know exactly what it means.

And what about the "bitches" and the "hos"? Well, a lot of this was covered in my first book. A lot of this could be handled by our women simply refusing to live down to that status. They've even taken to calling each other by these names, i.e., "What up, bitch" or "What up, ho". Once again, following us men down streets that we shouldn't even be on. I've never called a Black woman a bitch or a ho, and if a woman says I did, she may not be either of those things, but she would be a liar. Even though some may have tested my raising by pushing certain buttons, I've never crossed that line, especially with a black woman. Why? Because I was raised by a strong black woman. I was raised in a house with strong black women. I was raised around strong black women.

When I was coming up, if you called a black woman a bitch or a ho, you may as well head outside in the yard because there was about to be a fight. Win, lose or draw, she was going to fight you just so that you understood that she wasn't to be disrespected. What's sad these days is that they put up more of a fight for the right to be called such things. So the question remains, where does this leave me, the "nigga", and my black women, the "bitches" and the "hos"?

I don't blame hip hop entirely for what we see, although they are a large part of the problem. Robert De Niro is my favorite actor. How many times has he played an Italian mobster or criminal in films? Too many to count. Is he vilified for perpetuating that stereotype upon his people? No. In fact, he's celebrated as one of the greatest actors of all time, and rightfully so. And some of our hip hop artists, though degrading to women at times, are some of the greatest artist to ever step inside a recording booth. But we in the black community need to address how we address one another. Just because a woman is a little aggressive or exhibits some allegedly "bitchy" behavior, doesn't make her a bitch. Just because a woman exhibits some whorish behavior, doesn't make her a "ho", although she probably should check herself before the lie becomes the truth. There are circumstances surrounding all behavior and one should investigate and get all of the facts before making blanket statements about an individual or a group of people.

Hollywood, the white media or random talk show hosts should not feel that they're allowed to make those statements about our people just because we've been in their movies, on their TV shows or because they listen to our music. Isn't it enough that we're paraded around in front of white America on a daily basis on "reality" shows (and I strongly question the use of the term "reality"; how real are you when you know the cameras are rolling for your "audition"?) like *Flavor Of Love*, *I Love New York* and *College Hill*, where our women are literally prostituting themselves out on national TV? And what about talk shows like *The Jerry Springer Show*, that's showing how ignorant and promiscuous some black men and women can be? Not that these things are specific to blacks. Not only did we not invent promiscuity, we're far from cornering the market on it. All you have to do is look at Hollywood and how often they switch partners. Look at the Anna Nicole Smith tragedy and how many potential fathers her daughter allegedly had at the time of her death.

What black people are going through is what can be considered a family fight. If you're ever an outsider witnessing a family fight, it's always best to stay out of it. Sooner or later, a family fight is put to rest over a picnic and a glass of Kool-Aid. But what usually happens when the beef is squashed is they both wind up hating the outsider that got in their business. There's a long list of things that we as blacks need to stop doing to one another, and these words are on that list. But that doesn't mean that white people are allowed to say whatever they want about us until we fix it. When you're out buying your hip hop CD filled with these words, you're not buying the right to use those words towards us. You are buying a part of our culture, and though we appreciate your support, you should watch what you say to and about me (sorry, the East side of Detroit just showed up).

I am looking for a new revolution from our entertainers, both male and female, that puts a lot of these images to rest. But I don't need famous white folks who slip up one day and tell us how they really feel about us to pretend that the only reason they said it was because a rapper said it first. If you call us niggers and degrade our women, it's because that's how you feel about us, not because 50

Cent taught you that. You can't justify your hatred of my people by attempting to hold up a mirror to us. I heard a local radio host, who is white, say in reference to the Imus scandal—where the nationally syndicated radio host referred to the black players on the Rutgers University women's basketball team as "nappy headed hos"—that people shouldn't be so uptight about his use of the word "hos". "It just a word", he said. That tells me that, more than likely, "nigger" is just a word to him too.

If you don't understand the impact that words can have on a group of people or society as a whole, then you're bound to be just as ignorant as an Imus or Michael Richards is. What clowns like "Kramer", Imus the Terrible and any other white person that says these things on the air, in the open or behind closed doors must understand is that we may call each other bitches and hos and niggas all day, and we'll be over it by tomorrow. That's not right, but that's the way it is until we change it. But if someone from the other side says it, even if we were to find it in our hearts to forgive, we will never, ever forget.

Scene Four—A message to my people: "I know you're down, but when you gon' get up?"

Prayer For The Dying

Now I raise my hands to heaven and pray
Dear God, Dear God, don't let my thoughts go astray
If it be Thy will, end the suffering on earth
Purify my heart, and improve my worth
Not in the monetary, but as a spiritual being
Don't let me be corrupt by all the pain I've seen
For every disaster that occurs, please strengthen my heart
And if I falter in the middle, take me back to the start
Don't let me be confused by feelings of lost love
Thoughts of betrayal and anger, Lord, help me rise above
Lord, You know that I've longed for a love that's gone missing from me
But now I pray and pray for Your wisdom and strength, Lord teach me to let her be
I sought to satisfy my soul in the earthly sense
Now each night I pay with tears as this pillow I drench
And if it seems I've lost my focus, please don't charge my heart
This is a prayer for the dying, I wanna live a brand new start
When I awake from a grave of sorrow that despair has put me in
I'll shed the clothes of a broken man, let the new spirituality begin
I know I vowed not to pray selfishly the next time I came before You
But by praying for a spiritual awakening, Lord, I intend to be a man that's more true
True to You, true to life and more true to myself
And to forever be a seeker of more spiritual wealth
And if I'm a better servant, then society wins
'Cause I'm less likely to disappoint You with my continuous sins

Not saying I'd be perfect, but I'd be on the right path
No longer putting my faith in things that I know somehow won't last
I know You'll grant my every wish and all that my heart desires
You'll take me to the highest highs, and if I reach, You'll take me higher
I'm determined to make my dreams come true and it burns in me like a fire
You'll grant me the love of a good woman soon, one who nurtures, uplifts and inspires
This is a prayer for the dying as I bury my past, and I won't look back no more
One candle for God and one candle for me, may my life burn brighter than before

Are You Awake In This Life?

Are you awake in this life?
Or are you just sleepwalking?
Is your soul aligned with the heavens above?
Or in tune with the ways of the world?
Do you desire to be as the righteous among you?
Or do you run with the strays of the world?
In my quiet solitude
I'm alone with the thoughts of my mind
The silence in deafening
I close my eyes and begin to see
A collage of all my sins
Lying before me
I've dishonored my God with the path I've walked
Killed my brother with the poison I've sold
I've dishonored my wife and the vows we took
I've lied, I've cheated and I stole
My mind and my ways are that of the world
Though my soul set a path for spiritual redemption
In the flesh, I lost my way
Days and days wasted
Carnal conquests my only tasks
Continuing on in the ways of a fool
Irresponsibility thrown about my past
I can see the dawning of a brand new day
And yet I'm still asleep in my bed
Have I used my hands to do the work of the Father?
Or have I used them to destroy His land?
Yes, these are the questions that one must ask
Of himself and his fellow man
Has the potential of your life been completely realized?
Or have you succumb to the lust of the flesh?
And had your future compromised
By the firmness of her breasts
Or the natural curves of her hips
By the way he feels in the midnight hour
Or promises made from his lying lips

Are you really awake in this life?
Or do you have more time to waste
To continue on the path of selfishness and greed
And the almighty paper chase
Sometimes, no matter what you do
You can't outrun your past
'Cause in the end, no matter what you say
It's what you do that lasts
Everyday we have choices to make
Move forward or just keep still
Every promise made in immorality
Is a promise of that should go unfulfilled
We must distance ourselves from the sins we commit
And allow our souls to heal
And if there's a way to awake from my slumber
I promise you, I will
So …
Are you awake in this life?
Or are you just sleepwalking?

Just A Note From Your Jailor

… Just a note from your jailor
You'll never be free
You need to end your resistance
And completely embrace me

I'll completely suppress your will
And take away what you wanna be
You wanna break away, but it'll never happen
Just you wait and see

You can go where you wanna go
But never stray too far from me
I give you the illusion of freedom
But you'll never truly be free

Yeah, I monitor your every move
But there's really no need to react
You can go wherever you want, and do whatever you do
But you better be here when I get back

All I'm offering is protection
From all of the ills of the world
Just do what I say and follow all of my rules
And you'll always be my girl

Don't be concerned with the chains that I've placed on you life
It's not bondage, you'll always be free
The illusion of freedom is what you'll always enjoy
As long as you don't try to break free from me …

Ladies, the abuse isn't always physical …

Nigga Wasteland

My people are dying for leadership,
Yet they're aren't many leaders at hand
My people are dying from the drugs they take
In attempts to make the mind expand

Come walk with me down my mama's street
And take me by the hand
Walk with me as we travel to
What's called the nigga wasteland

How can we ever expect to succeed
Without ever having a plan?
400 plus years escaping the oppressor's whip
And the evil portrayed by the man

Nowadays we smoking blunts and cookin' coke
Instead of grits in our pots and pans
And all of that sex without a condom
Won't ever be a good health plan

Crack addicts and AIDS victims litter the 'hood
As our death toll quickly expands
All so some nigga can have a fancy car
And rule the nigga wasteland

By the words of many a hip hop star
We out the 'hood, so let's drink and dance
Weighed down by diamonds and 24-inch rims
I simply don't understand

Black boys and black girls
Black woman and man
Our souls are priceless above rubies and gold
And cars that cost 200 grand

Our children are steadily dying
Killed by our own hands
Never see your daughter grow into a woman
Never see your son as a man

Give me a hundred matches
And some gas in a can
And watch me set fire and burn to the ground
This nigga wasteland

My people are dying for leadership
Yet, there aren't any leaders at hand
I'm trying to earn a spot at the front of the line
And throw life preservers to the black man

Let's organize a march on our own neighborhoods
Let no work of iniquity stand
Bring rebirth to the black man's spirit
And death to the nigga wasteland

My Hypocrisy

It's time I break the chain of destruction
And choose the path of wisdom and right
I must distance myself from the man in the street
Because we're both too much alike

I have too much in common with the sinful man
We are one and we share the same highs
I don't have the ability to look down on him
'Cause we still see eye to eye

I tell him about the wrong he does everyday
About the changes he needs to make in his life
Yet I share a drink with him and I curse twice as much
And like him, I'll cheat on my wife

My brothers are falling each day in the 'hood
Yet you'll never ever see me cry
Instead, I just bury my head in the sand
And pretend that I don't know why

I go to church on Sundays and pray real hard
But it never seems to be enough
So by Monday I'm back to my old ways again
More marijuana smoke to puff

Where's my leadership from the darkened path?
How am I an example for change?
When I participate in that which I deplore
It's myself that I strain to explain

I must embrace the brand new and release the old
Break the slave chains and be set free
Move on to the future and bury my past
In the bottom of the deep blue sea

I must dive deep into the holiest of waters
And give my soul a bath
I must allow God to heal my spiritual blindness
And shine a light down upon my path

I must give and give from the depths of my soul
I must give much more than most
'Cause I'm trying my best to earn my wings
And heaven is oh so close

Everyday you're alive you make history
You make footprints in the cement of life
So bring roses from your concrete and take advantage of God's grace
Before life's sunshine turns to night

I must be a brand new creature with a purposeful life
Take my place as a leader of men
No longer be a part of the destruction I see
And bring my hypocrisy to an end

A Few Dirty Words

You see her at the mall just about every weekend
No money in her pocket, but she won't quit seekin'
The right outfit to make all the boys stare
Rather than using the mind 'cause it's just not there
You peep her from the food court, plottin' your game
You wanna go beyond simply "What's your name"
But it ain't that hard if you wanna know the half
She got no interest in taking time, 'cause she's much too fast
Tonight is always the night 'cause she hates to be alone
And with a few dirty words, you can take her home
You see her at the club on the very next week
Out with her girls in the mood to freak
You don't know that she's here almost every weekend
Over at the bar posted up with her friends
You gotta approach with respect, on the surface it seems
But every drink she takes evaporates self esteem
You better make your move before another brotha will
'Cause he's a freak vet and he knows how she feels
Go over and take her hand 'cause you look so fly
You'll come to realize you already caught her eye
She's feeling your outfit 'cause she's so, so shallow
No pride exists inside because she's oh so hollow
But nobody can tell her nothing 'cause she'll tell you she's grown
And with a few dirty words, you'll be takin' her home
As you walk to your car, she's texting your cell
Pretending that she's shy, but you know her too well
Telling you that she don't normally do this
But on the first night, she wants to meet for a kiss
Tells her girls she gotta go 'cause work is early in the morning
But in 30 to 45 she'll be on her back moanin'
She follows you to the crib and you've seen it before
Pretend to talk outside, soon you're headed for the door
Your hands on her body and she's begging for more
While all the while sayin' she's never done this before

But we both know she's lyin' 'cause she seems like a pro
And in few dirty words she'll be ready to go
'Cause no matter what she says, her body's in charge
Plus she's drunk again, another excuse to go too far
She swears she's not a ho, but what the hell are we doing?
You barely know this man and there's about to be screwing
But just block it out of your mind and pretend you're a queen
You're not a fool if no one knows, do you know what I mean?
You don't have to fool her 'cause she fools herself
And if it wasn't you tonight, it would've been someone else
She doesn't seem to mind when she acts like a whore
And with a few dirty words, she'll be on the floor
She'll let you do to her body whatever you will
She'd tell you how much she likes it, but she's too drunk to feel
Send her home in the morning, still drunk off Absolut
Panties in her purse like a prostitute
Don't call her for four days and it pisses her off
'Cause she thought you shared something and now she feels lost
She gave you her body 'cause she thought you cared
Or at least that's what it seems when the drinks ain't there
What's infatuation to us, to her it's love
That's what makes her give her body to any and every scrub
But because you hit and ran, she swears she's over you
Now she's gonna seek God and stop being a fool
No more drinks, no more sex and she's changing her friends
Yeah, right …
Just a few dirty words and she'll be back again

Not my girl ...

If this phone rings again, I swear I won't answer
'Cause she won't let go, she's a sickness like cancer
Took her to the room, made her my private dancer
Now I wanna get away 'cause some days, I can't stand her
Got all of her attention 'cause she liked my rims
So easy to take advantage of a mind so dim
Every couple weeks our so-called love is to an end
And I won't call her back until I'm horny again
If you wanna push up, be my guest, it ain't no thang
But be sure that you're sure 'cause every brotha can't hang
She won't give you love 'cause that's not what she do
And if you ain't got the money she'll be through with you
I just get up in between when she gives me the chance
But no kissing in public, excessive huggin' or holding hands
She's pretending that she's deep, but I know the deal
She swears she's in love, but that ain't what I feel
She's not my girl, I just play with her mind
Get what I want and leave her ass behind
She stays for my status and she loves my style
Even though another brotha might be worth her while
He might treat her right and show her much respect
He may actually care that she has feelings to protect
He might give her more than just a wine and dine
He might appreciate more than just her big behind
That spiritual side of her, he may be willing to feed
But she thinks she loves me, so that's all I need
He might be more willing to give her the time of day
'Cause she can't get that if she's coming my way
When she dials my number sex is all I play
And if I flash enough cash, she'll do what I say
Let another brotha try to show the respect she needs
She'll just shut his ass down and come runnin' back to me
She's convinced that she needs me while he tell her she don't
Praying that she'll listen, but I know she won't
But she's not my girl, so I really don't care
And the next time I call, she'll be right there

So, why are women more willing to be played by a man of alleged status, than to be taken care of by a man of principle? A question in need of an answer …

Mama's Eyes

"Be still", mama said as she combed my hair. "We've got to be perfect this time". It's opening night again, and we gotta put on a good performance. That's what mama says. My clothes is smelling real good today. It smells like that fabric softener stuff. Mama's really nervous right now. She's been like that all day. I couldn't go out and play today 'cause she said I would get dirty. I really wanted to go, but I would get a whippin' if I talked back. Mama said today is really important for us. She said it's important for the rest of our lives. "Sit down on the couch and don't mess up your clothes", she said. "4:00 will be here soon".

I love my mama a lot, but sometimes I don't understand her. Like, some days she hugs me a lot and tells me she loves me. And sometimes her eyes look really weird and she locks herself in her room. Then, sometimes when I go to sleep she seems really happy, but when I wake up for school the next day she seems really sad. She drives me to school sometimes with shades on, even when there's no sun outside. When I ask what's wrong, she says "Mommy's having trouble with her eyes today, but you shouldn't be in grown folk's business". But I don't think I'm in grown folk's business. She's my mama and I love her. I just wanna know what's wrong. Sometimes at night, I hear her crying and it wakes me up. When I go to her room and I look in, I see her on the floor. One time her mouth was bleeding. One time it was her eye. It makes me sad, so I go back to my room and I cry 'til I fall asleep. Sometimes I wanna hold my mama, but I go back to my room. Mama says I should never come into her room or I'm gonna get a whippin'.

Sometimes I see men in the house. Some of them I remember, but most of them are strangers to me. The one I remember the most lives in our neighborhood, I think. I think he does 'cause I see him sometimes when I'm outside playing. He drives by the house in his shinny truck. "What up, lil man", he says sometimes. I just wave. One time he came by, and my mama came out. She gave him some money and he put something in her hand. I don't know what it was 'cause it was too small to see. I wanted to ask, but I remembered what mama said about grown folk's business. But still, I wish I knew why he be in our house sometimes. 'Cause sometimes when I see him and he leaves, one way or another, mama's eyes end up looking wrong.

It's almost 4:00. Mama is getting more and more nervous. She's in the bathroom right now. She's putting on make-up. Her eyes have been dark. It looks like she's covering them up with the make-up. She looks really pretty when her eyes ain't dark. She put on a long sleeved shirt today. I think she's ashamed of her arms. They got a lotta marks on them. When she sees me looking at them, she says that mommy's sick. I don't think I know what that means, but she says that she'll be better soon. "It's almost Showtime baby, are you ready?" mommy asked me. "I guess so", I said. I don't know what else I'm supposed to say. "Mommy's gonna get you a daddy today", she said. "But you gotta be good or he'll run away", she said. She looks like she's gonna cry. But I don't say anything. "This time, he gon' stay", mama says.

Then, somebody knocked on the door. "Go get the door baby", mama said. She really sounded nervous. "Don't forget to look out the window first to see who it is", she says. When I looked out the window, I saw the shinny truck. I opened the door. "What up, lil man", he said through the screen door. "Where yo' mama at?", he asked. I opened the screen door and he came in. "Hey daddy", mama said. She seemed really excited. "What up", he said. "Let's go in the back", he said to mama. "Okay", mama said. But now she don't look happy. She look sad again. "Sit down and watch TV 'til I come back", mama said. So I sit on the couch. I keep hearing noises from the back. At first, it sounds like mama was crying. Then it stopped. I don't know what to do, so I better keep watching TV. He's coming out now, but he only been here for a few minutes. He look like he sweatin' "Later, lil man" he says to me. I want to know if mama is okay. I'm gonna go in the back to see her. I'm looking in her room and mama has her back to me. "Mama, are you alright?" I ask. She turned around and looked at me. Mama's eyes looked bad again.

Hard To Breathe

Look outside your window and tell me what you see
Is the world we know in disarray?
Has poverty, homelessness and a sense of despair
Come to your neighborhood to stay?

It's getting harder and harder to breathe out here
This ghetto fog is way too strong
And in my efforts to try and change the tune of this song
I always wind up singing along

I wanna exhale and give my lungs a break
I've been holding this for way too long
But instead, I inhale all the poison in the sky
Until all my sensibility is gone

I see my brothers on the corner with their lives on hold
Pushing danger through the neighborhood
Their minds spinning like the rims they aspire to get
I wanna believe they'd break the cycle if they could

We swing limb from limb in the concrete jungle
So afraid of where we might land
As the drugs and the alcohol and the genocide
Replace the dreams that now slip from our hands

Black ghetto girl with the weight of the world
On her shoulders and she just can't take it
She heads down to the club and strips for her money
'Cause she don't know how else to make it

The paper chase has blinded us like rage blinds a killer
Like envy, our eyes have turned green
Educated fools, brains and souls both lacking
As we live outside of our means

Meager accommodations are not quite good enough
God is speaking, but we can't hear the sound
We don't praise Him for the things that we already have
As the homeless sleep on the cold, cold ground

Deep in the 'hood we're all under pressure
'Cause everyday we know we gotta fight
Gotta always be ready to get down on the ground
'Cause in the ghetto, gun blasts takes lives

I just wanna run away but there's no where to run to
And if I run, I'll never be free
And no matter how far away from here I go
This will always be home to me

I know we all down, but how gon' get up?
It's getting harder and harder to believe
That we ever gon' make it with the hands of the ghetto
'Round our necks …
… and we still can't breathe …

The Man Behind The Mask

Who is the man behind the mask?
Who is the man that's afraid of his past?
He knows no freedom, for the mask is his cage
It hides his fears, his tears and conceals his rage
His mask hides the pain that would be evident in his face
Past sins pursue his soul, so he picks up the pace
Who is the man behind the mask?
Who is the man that prays his pain won't last?
He's a man too deep in the ways of the earth
A man that struggles to define his worth
His mask is a smile that misleads the masses
Yet the pain inside increases as each moment passes
It's the pain felt from lost love and missed opportunity
It's pain that he feels from his people's lack of unity
He's a man that doesn't understand that he must embrace his past
Lest it consume him and cut him down like blades of grass
He's a man too consumed with protecting his pride
So instead, he commits emotional suicide
This life he's lived hasn't gone as planned
So he prays for more clarity 'cause he just don't understand
That the sins of the past are the sins of the past
You must cleanse your soul so that you can remove your mask
Let the world see your face so that all can see
Just how wonderful the mercy of God can be

Somebody Send Some Help ...

Wish I could do something to change the atmosphere
My eyes so bloodshot, that I can't see clear
Can't leave my kids outside 'cause we livin' in fear
Somebody send some help 'cause we dyin' out here
I'm undereducated so my job's no good
The government promised help and I wish they would
I can't feed my family so I steal at night
I wanna go to church but they don't treat me right
My baby mama pregnant by the preacher man
My sister smoke crack and her babies don't understand
I'd leave the 'hood tomorrow if I had a plan
But my weed smokin' destroyed the life it was supposed to enhance
Alienated by my family but I really need 'em near
Somebody send some help 'cause we dyin' out here
Determined every day to give life one more try
But I wind up finding new ways to get high
Believing the white man's lie that's it's just in my blood
The undying desire for alcohol and drugs
I can't change my DNA, but I can change my choices
When the demons speak to me, I should ignore the voices
But I can't make it alone, I need help with this
Wish somebody thought I was worth the risk
Wish somebody would come along to dry our tears
Somebody send some help 'cause we dyin' ...

To My People

My eyes well up with tears
As I weep for the confusion of my people
Who have turned their eyes away from God
And embraced all forms of evil

Choosing the ways of the streets
Where death is the only solution
We've inhaled the knowledge of our forefathers
But breathed it out into the air as pollution

We've been armed with enough power
To cause this earth to shift
But because we turned our eyes away from the Father
We've continued to lose our grip

We've embraced all the negativity
That our ancestors fought against for years
We continuously disrespect our mothers
As we watched our fathers disappear

We place ourselves in bondage
Yet we complain that we'll never be free
Never fully understanding the meaning of freedom
And it's responsibility

We don't know the difference between a prosperous life
And one where we're simply rich
We don't know the difference between what we want and what's right
And don't have the wisdom to tell which from which

What good is having all of this paper
If I can't match each dollar with knowledge?
What good is 24's on my Escalade
If I can't put my son through college?

Why can't I get a sister to love me for me
When I promise to always be true?
Why does it seem that she only loves me
When I bruise her black and blue?

How many times will I have to be down
Before I can't get up one mo' time?
Why must I continue to sacrifice my soul
When salvation seems too hard to find?

Wish I could meet Jesus and touch that garment
Let Him spiritually medicate me
Give me the wisdom and knowledge that I so crave
Bring unity to me and the streets

Help me make a better way for black folks 'round here
Keep the street lights on 'til we're home safe
Grandparents on our blocks are still living in fear
After years of fighting to make a better way

For ungrateful people like me and my crew
I don't know when we ever gon' learn
Maybe when we're rejected at the gates of heaven
On our way to that permanent burn

It's time to create a brand new day
Where my people failing at life seems strange
To the youth that'll lead the next generation
… I ask …
Are you really ready for change?

Dance With The Devil

As the night time finds me
I'm feeling all alone
As my dark thoughts bind me
I need to find my way home

To a place where my spirit
Has a resting place
But when the dark calls, I hear it
And yet I feel no disgrace

It's the sound of angel
But he's the angel of sin
He's not my Father's angel
But he's says I can win

If I dance with the devil
I'll see riches untold
He wants to bring me to his level
In exchange for my soul

Should I dance with the devil?
I'm just a child of the sun
Will all my work with The Father
Become completely undone?

As he approaches me slowly
He takes the form of a man
Then he whispers to me lowly
And he extends to me his hand

"All you want can be yours"
He says to me with a smile
"I can open all the doors
I can accentuate your style"

"If you just believe in me
I can take your fears away
I know you long to be free
Just follow me, I know the way"

And now my eyes are filled with tears
'Cause it seems he knows me well
He brings a calm to all my fears
He seems to know how much I've failed

At being righteous and true
To my convictions and beliefs
So now I don't know what to do
I need a way to just release

Then I danced with the devil
I'm just a child of the sun
And my work with The Father
Quickly becomes undone

Now, I'm knee deep in the life
Embracing all that he gives
With my riches comes strife
And darkness is where I live

My life is lived in the night
Because I sleep in the day
Some kind of vampire life
Is what I live in a way

This is the life that he promised me
In exchange for my soul
But this is not what I wanna be
While my soul grows old

I couldn't see that I was free
Before he made me a slave
There's nothing wrong with being me
In the light The Father gave

Now I'm mired in self-pity
Now I'm mired in sin
As I cry out in the city
There's only one way to win

Break my dance with the devil
And be a child of The Son
I must repent to The Father
And bring together what's undone

As I kneel down to pray
Tears stream down my face
As I wish the pain away
I knew I never could replace

All the love of The Father
How could I ever be so blind?
I simply made it all much harder
I have to leave it all behind

I wanna meet with the dark one
But we shall dance no more
I wanna tell him that we're all done
Because The Father gives me more

Much more than I realized
But gratitude wasn't there
Now misery has opened my eyes
Now I feel Him everywhere

The dark one now shows surprise
'Cause to his fire, I am cold
I look him right in his eyes
As I reconnect with my soul

He didn't think I could reclaim
What he tricked me into giving
He didn't think I could regain
The soul I lost through sinful living

I'll give it back to The King
I'll send it home where it belongs
I now regret everything
And all the right I turned to wrong

I shouldn't have danced with the devil
'Cause I'm a child of The Son
Now I'm repairing with Father
All the work that's been undone

Don't dance with the devil
'Cause he seeks to steal your soul
Just when you think you're on his level
Your life has spun out of control

Don't let him make you believe
That you should give your soul to him
Don't let him make you believe
That without him, you can't win

Don't be a victim of the dark side
When he whispers, tune deaf ears
'Cause to the bottom, it's a long slide
And he'll control your soul for years

Just put your faith in The Father
Trust me, it's the only way
Don't seek to make your life darker
Try to seek a brighter day

Never dance with the devil
'Cause we're children of The Son
Continue working with The Father
Until all your work is done

A Prayer To Black Jesus

This morning I hit my knees and prayed to Black Jesus
Asking Him to save my people today
I asked Him to wash all of our sins away
I asked Him to show us a better way
I prayed and I prayed for the inspiration
Of the underdeveloped and lazy mind
I prayed and I prayed for relief from desperation
And liberation from the black man's crimes
The next MLK has already been born
Probably living in my neighborhood
But he's stuck and mired in addiction's mud
And he'd lead us out of if he could
How can he organize a march on the very streets
That he helped to contaminate?
How can he turn away all the corruption he meets
When it promises him a better way?
As I continued my conversation with Black Jesus
He revealed some things to me
There's only so much of his freedom that a man can exercise
If he's really to remain free
Discipline is a necessary prison to have
So lock yourself up and throw away the key
Disconnect the shackles of the street's materialism
And connect yourself to morality
The next Malcolm X has already been born
The next Frederick Douglass, too
Black Jesus told me He's provided us a way out
The question is, what do we plan to do?
As I concluded my prayer I thanked the Lord for His blessings
Yet, He had a request for me
He said …
"My son, when you get off your knees this time
Be the leader that you think we need"

Slave Days

Slave days is over, I thought you heard
We overcame the cotton fields, you should spread the word
You can't make me bow to your wicked system
You try to hold him down, but the Spirit lifts him
You try to break that spirit, but I'm way too strong
You try to shorten my knowledge, but its way too long
I was raised by people that walked the dirt roads
Way before my arrival they were lifting the heavy loads
From the back roads of Georgia, they made it through
So your concrete jungle's nothing for me to do
You push your criticism thinking I'm gon' move
But I've already won, I have nothing to prove
My mind's eye shows me the cotton fields
Where my people slaved by day and at night they kneeled
Praying to the Lord for my safe arrival
Their perseverance is what taught me about survival
I was conceived in the mind before I made it here
By people who were constantly living in fear
Of the oppressor's whip and his rapist ways
Would've been born into captivity had Tubman not strayed
Fast forward to today and the system you run
You think I'll ever let you win when the day is done?
Extend the financial carrot to keep me under control
You'll give me all I want in exchange for my soul
But if I learn to adapt to your wicked ways
You'll take me back hundreds of years, back to the slave days
But I got too much pride and respect for my past
To be a part of a system that I know won't last
Build your fortunes on my back, but at the end of the day
Retribution's coming soon and you'll be forced to pay
Now that we're physically free, you want a mental slave
You want more blood from me, but my people already gave
We found our voice in those cotton fields when we sang of being free
And though some will conform, a house nigga I won't be
I'll break the chains that were first broken in those cotton fields
Others may bow, but you'll never make me kneel

Awake

Let your voice be the voice of inspiration
For those that need to be inspired
Let your desire to treat others as you'd want to be treated
Be the strongest of all your desires

I wish I could take away the ills of society
For the sake of my unborn child
I wish I could do away with the helplessness we feel
As our children continue to run wild

We've foolishly forgotten that we should always pray
Believing that it does no good
But it's the only thing that will stop all the funeral processions
That keep riding through our neighborhoods

This life you live is a gift from God
A gift that was meant to last
Yet reckless living accelerates our journey
To the graveyards that lie within our paths

Our struggles in life will take us to places
We're not sure we want to go
But all of the rain that falls in our lives
Causes flowers of character to grow

Let not your days here on earth be defined
By all the money you burn
But rather let them be defined by all the knowledge
And wisdom you have earned

Let your soul be a light that shines
Bright enough to light your way
Awake from the slumber that immorality put you under
Awake to a brand new day

Redemption

Are you ready to embrace your redemption today?
Are you ready for the blessings that'll come your way?
We were promised much more than what we see on earth
None of which was meant to define our worth
Redemption's on the horizon, but if you can't see
Then you'll deny yourself that which will make you free
We seem unaware that Jesus saves
In the midst of devastation and Katrina's waves
I stand before you boldly in the name of Christ
Urging you to let Him take control of your life
Do it before your day time suddenly turns to night
And I promise that He'll make everything alright
Redemption is waiting for you to sing its song
Time is growing short, so don't wait too long
It's a song of hope in the midst of rain clouds
It brings strength to weak and more empowerment to the proud
It represents hope and uplifts us all
It encourages you to stand when others may fall
No more dying time, now it's time to live
Time to live out the promise that redemption gives …

Scene Five—KJ's Inspiration: Closing Act

To My Unborn Daughter

By the time you read these words
You will have come to understand
That just your mere presence is a blessing to me
You've made your father a better man

I've foreseen your birth for years
All the joy that a daughter can bring
I've prayed for your success in life
More than I've prayed for anything

I hope to watch you grow
Into a beautiful Swan
If my life is filled with the darkness of night
You represent the dawn

I'm afraid this world has changed so much
That I don't know if we should bring you here
But I've prayed that God will keep his arms around you
And that removes all doubt and fear

I can't wait to see your beautiful smile
And hold you in my arms
I can't wait to sit you on my knee
As you disarm me with your charm

You'll warm the hearts of many
You'll touch the hearts of man
Your life will be filled with blessings
You'll be touched by the Master's hand

May your life represent the lyrics
To one of God's most beautiful compositions
Remember to carry yourself with pride
And a graceful disposition

I see the uniqueness of you
You soar above the clouds
You are destined for greatness
I know that you'll make me proud

When I think of you, I'm happy
I begin to beam with pride
'Cause you are your daddy's Princess
You're the apple of his eye

Beware of the pitfalls of life
This world will try to tear you down
So let your dreams reach beyond the stars
But keep your feet planted on the ground

Whatever challenges you face
Be sure to be up to the test
And whatever you decide to do with your life
Be sure to give it your best

There'll be times when this world will tempt you
There'll be times when the road gets hard
So be careful not to put your faith in man
And remember to place it in God

Though women have changed these days
Giving up their divinity without a fight
I'll do what I can to arm you with knowledge
I'll do my best to raise you right

Always try to do the right thing
Love yourself more than anyone else
Remember what it means to be a lady
And remember to respect yourself

Because many will say that they love you
But they aren't necessarily being true
So be sure to follow the light of God
And you'll always know just what to do

Keep your mind focused on your goals
And no matter what you do
Know that your daddy loves you
And he'll lay down his life for you

KJ In Progress … (A letter to my big brother)

Dear Paul,

These are the written words of a soul that's in progress
Moving through pain, bitterness and a touch of happiness
Never knew what my purpose should be in life
Never thought I have to do it without you telling me right
Everyday since I lost you, you've stayed on my mind
Only the good memories, the rest I've left behind
I'm hoping that you approve of the path I chose
Trying to steer clear of the pitfalls in life, I've tried to stay in control
17 years and sometimes I still ain't right
Sometimes my eyes still cry in the middle of the night
Yet I'm doing my best to make you proud of me
Show off to the angels what I've come to be
Everyday my work here is less of a mystery
Look in my face, my big brother's still living through me
When you first left me here, I'm thinking life ain't fair
How can I go on when I know you're not there
But I know I made it through because of mama's prayers
Now protection's all around me, I feel it everywhere
My soul is still in progress though the journey's sometimes rough
I'm trying to be the better man, but sometimes that's not enough
I've made mistakes along the way that I wish I could take back
But I never let it break me, I always got back on track
You got another nephew, he's blessed with the looks we share
Dark like us, smiles like us, and sometimes he don't seem to care
He carries our nonchalant nature well
I'll try to guide him as you did us in hopes that he'll never fail
I fell in love a few times with some girls that were no good
I wanted to steer clear of heartbreak, but somehow I don't think I could
I've avoided the lure of the streets as you always told me I should
Though the streets you knew have changed, it's a completely different 'hood
But don't you worry 'bout me 'cause I'm never scared
Can't wait to see you again, but now I'm not prepared
I've still got a lot of work that has to be done
Gotta be here for mama, gotta raise my son

Those are things you taught me before you left me here
So I step up to the plate without hesitation or fear
We'll be together soon, it's not an "if" but rather a "when"
Continue to guide me on the straight and narrow until we meet again

Your baby brother,
KJ

About the Author

Kelly R. Jackson has been an author/poet for over 20 years. You could say his writing career began in 11th grade when as a shy 16 year old, he wrote a poem about a girl in one of his classes. He would never get up the nerve to speak to this young lady, much less share with her what he wrote, but from that moment on, he's been writing. He spent 7 years working in the field of television production and he published his first book, *Temporarily Disconnected*, in 2006. He's also the proud father of one son, Steffen. He is a native of Detroit, Michigan, where he still resides, and he is a member of Zion Hill Baptist Church.

To contact Kelly R. Jackson, to read more of his work or to give feedback on any of his projects, visit www.kjworldonline.com or email him at kjworld@kjworldonline.com.

978-0-595-44964-4
0-595-44964-6

Printed in the United States
80225LV00003B/202-249